Ultimate Internet Marketing Strategies and Tactics for Turbulent Times

Dr Michael Teng
Ms Janelle Teng

Published in 2009 by
Corporate Turnaround Centre Pte Ltd.

Printed in Singapore
by Markono Print Media Pte Ltd.

9 8 7 6 5 4 3 2 1
09   10

Contents

Introduction to the authors

Dr. Mike Teng

Dr. Teng is widely recognized as a turnaround CEO in Asia by the news media. He has been interviewed on the international media on many occasions on the subject of corporate turnaround and transformation such as the Malaysian Business Radio, BFM 89-9, News Radio FM 93.8, Malaysian Business Radio, Edge Radio (USA), the Channel News Asia, the Boss Magazine, Economic Bulletin, the Today, World Executive Digest, Lianhe ZaoPao, StarBiz and the Straits Times.

Dr. Mike Teng is the author of a best-selling book *"Corporate Turnaround: Nursing a sick company back to health"*, in 2002 which is also translated into the Bahasa Indonesia. His book is endorsed by management guru Professor Philip Kotler and business tycoon, Mr. Oei Hong Leong. He subsequently authored more than ten management books.

Dr. Teng is currently the Managing Director of Corporate Turnaround Centre Pte Ltd (*www.corporateturnaroundcentre.com*) which provides corporate training and management advisory services. He has more than 29 years of experience in distributorship management, strategic planning and operational management responsibilities in the Asia Pacific. Of these, he held Chief Executive Officer's positions for 18 years in multi-national and publicly listed companies. He spearheaded the turnaround of several troubled companies as the CEO and also advised several boards of directors of numerous distressed companies.

Dr. Teng served as the Executive Council member for fourteen years and the last four years as the President of the Marketing Institute of Singapore (2000 – 2004), the national marketing association. He was on the advisory board member to Business School, National University of Singapore and Schoolof

Business, Singapore Polytechnic as well as the Doctoral Program, University of South Australia.

Dr. Teng holds a Doctor in Business Administration (DBA) from the University of South Australia, Master in Business Administration (MBA) and Bachelor in Mechanical Engineering (BEng) from the National University of Singapore. He is also a Professional Engineer (P Eng, Singapore), Chartered Engineer (C Eng, UK) and Fellow Member of several prestigious professional institutes namely, Chartered Institute of Marketing (FCIM), Chartered Management Institute (FCMI), Institute of Mechanical Engineers (FIMechE), Marketing Institute of Singapore (FMIS), Institute of Electrical Engineers (FIEE) and Senior Member of Singapore Computer Society (SMSCS). He is also a Practising Management Consultant (PMC) certified by the Singapore government.

Ms. Janelle Teng

Ms. Janelle Teng is the founder and sole-proprietor of a business dealing in the sale of Star Wars memorabilia (*www.starwarcard.com*). She is the daughter of Dr. Michael Teng. Her business focuses primarily on the sale of out-of-print Star Wars: Customizable Card Game cards, but also sources and purchases rare memorabilia from around the world for clients as part of a personalized shopping service. Her client base includes many collectors and professional Star Wars: Customizable Card Game players from Europe and the United States. Ms. Teng established her business after graduating from Raffles Junior College, where she achieved straight As in her A-Level examinations. She is a self-taught businesswoman, and her natural business acumen and street smarts have allowed her entrepreneurship venture to grow from a simple card shop into the international enterprise that it is today via the Internet.

Introduction

Today, the Internet has paved the way for an entirely new universe full of opportunities for even the most insignificant business owner who is home-based. There are many successful self-made millionaires who utilized Internet intelligently to achieve success. The newly-minted rich are no different than we. They began their Internet companies from the ground floor, found a niche for themselves and meticulously worked on to achieve success.

"Is it really possible to make money using the Internet?"

The truth is -- you can make real money using the Internet – lots of it. You simply have to take the right steps for it to happen. You need a sincere determination to achieve your goal and the right attitude. Those who have passion for their business, will.

The secret of developing a successful Internet-based business is strong determination. Many of the entrepreneurs fail precisely when they are just about to attain success.

Why? They simply lack the drive needed for success and quit.

If you keep trying, it is impossible to fail.

Closing the gate. (Ultimate internet strategy)

Shout it from the roof tops, shout it from the schools

That you have to use the web, or you'll be a fool

There is no way forward, other than using our brains

There is only stagnation, and nasty, horrible pain

The world is travelling, on a bumpy, economic slide

The world is unravelling, don't get lost on the ride

Tell the students in universities, and big business owners

We have to utilise the web, because there are no money donors

The waves are crashing, and breaking against the shore,

You do not seem convinced, let me tell you some more,

The web has influence and power, like the force in Star Wars

The web can give you riches, just don't get drunk in bars.

For you are wasting your time, trying to think like the old days

You need to restructure your lines, and think into ways that pay

New ways of marketing will get your message heard,

Don't be fooled by security, don't get lost with the herd

You're better than you think you are, you're better than the pack

But you can't get lazy or crazy, you have to pick up the slack

The world waits for no man, so get killer copy writing,

The world waits for no woman, and this is where it gets exciting

Credibility is everything, targeting traffic the ideal

Professional websites and passion, will keep things real

Making money this way, will pull us out of this recession

Making money like this will stop us reverting in regression.

So teach this to the students, teach this to all the kids

That by using these methods, will stop us hitting the skids

New ways of working have to be respected, and learned,

The new ways of working, will stop us getting burned.

So get a good quality product, and sell it to the masses,

Before we're out of a job, and the stock market crashes,

If we act now before it's too late, we can avoid a fate

Where we have no work, as someone has closed the gate!

Here is the list of the most important factors that one may need for attaining Internet marketing success:

A True and Sincere Zeal

To succeed, you need passion for your business. If you lack true passion, you cannot achieve the success you are looking for.

Your personal Domain (for example: www.yourspecificdomain.com)

If you host your business using a free server it is rarely considered seriously. They tend to be thought of as unprofessional. A company that does not care enough for an exclusive domain name might not be able to attract customers who feel confident on doing business there. A company having an exclusive domain name and a professional looking website is likely to have a significantly higher success rate compared to the majority business sites that are hosted using free servers.

Professional Website

Your site is a direct reflection of your attitude, personality, and the business you have created. Designing a professional looking site with a purpose of making sales takes a great deal of effort and time, seeing that there are other factors beyond the design of the website. You need to look at the big picture and intentionally design your website to sell.

Informative, good quality Content

If you wish to create a constant flow of traffic, you need to give your visitors something that would attract them to your site frequently. Just one visit is not enough to maintain a business. You need to keep your visitors informed and entertained with new content on a regular basis.

Focused and Targeted Traffic

Regardless of how good your website is, if you are not getting high-quality, authentic traffic you cannot succeed. Your website could get 'n' number of visitors each day; but if none of them are interested in the service or products you offer, your web traffic is useless for you. You have to encourage and receive continual, targeted traffic on your website.

Opt-in List (Ezine)

Creating your personally designed publication is an essential for success. This provides you direct contact with probable customers and will also allow you to sponsor goods and services as well as create credibility.

Your Own In-Demand Product

Marketing affiliate programs might provide good income, but the real profits come from marketing a product of your own which you know is in demand.

Killer Sales Copy

We know pens are mightier than swords! The words you create are the reflection of your personality. The product, design of the website and well-planned marketing strategies all hinge on what you have to say. You should know how to write a sales letter that can persuade your desired customers. You need to empathize with your customers' needs. This will direct you to create the letter with passion, enthusiasm, and advantage.

Killer Marketing Strategy

Creating a killer strategy is vital for the success of your online business. For succeeding, you will have to develop and follow a strategy throughout that includes the following:

- A great product

- A website specifically developed to sell the product or service

- A fool proof marketing strategy

And, remember, all these together can ensure you the SUCCESS!

Instantaneous Product Delivery (Ensure: fast download, instant access, easy navigation, simple look etc.)

People surf Internet for finding information. The users wish to find out the info they are looking for. The best products for the buyer in the Internet are the one that is delivered instantly.

Accept Credit Cards

When you conduct business over the Internet, it is imperative that you accept credit cards. You need to provide visitors with a simple online ordering process that they can follow and the convenience to pay for their order online. You can also set up an account with a third party such as PayPal.

Developing Credibility

For an Internet-based entrepreneur it is important to ensure that his or her visitors feel comfortable with the vendor and with the website. So, to get your visitor's confidence and trust, you have to build your credibility. Your attitude is a pivotal factor in shaping your success. You need to remain optimistic and be always ready to face any challenge that you might have along the way. The truth is that you are able do whatever you please. You just need to believe that 'you can' and most importantly, 'believe in yourself'.

Presence

Classified ads could determine your success. There is no reason to belittle this option.

A majority of people spend considerable time offline and you must utilize this time. If you have a physical presence or location, make sure you do the following:

• Put out signs that attract users. The words that lead most of the users are Find us on here....in the Internet and the ideal Search Engine Friendly URL will be "www.myspecificdomain.com".

• Have a catalog available online that helps the customer to look and shop.

• Print your email address and website on everything: brochures, business cards, cash register tape, invoices, letterhead, packing lists, and other related publicity options.

• If you are the first business in your specific area or field to establish online presence, it is simple to publish an article in your local newspaper to inform about your presence. Be in touch with the newspaper that covers stories on new business. If you find the right person/correspondent at the local trade magazine, you could publish some write-up on your business.

• Disburse press releases to your local magazines that you think that are read by your target audience. If your business features in the "what's new" column you will be able attract local users' attention.

• Should you be able to gather the funds, keep a computer in your store. You can also think of putting up a booth at a trade show to allow your customers to visit your site.

• Set up a virtual tour of your business on your website.

• If you have the email of your buyers, you can send them mails announcing a special offering, sale, or to just remind them of your shop and business. If you have customers without an email address, you can fax or post a monthly newsletter that list items that are up for sale.

CHAPTER ONE: Direct Sales

1.A Sales Letters

The following five strategies (plus an optional sixth) for writing sales letters have been instrumental in online success whether for my own product or that of someone else as a proxy.

1. Create Hope

Scores of people search for hope every day. People look to buy money-making e-books, diet e-books, how-to-gamble e-books and many more based solely on hope. Ninety-nine per cent of these people do not put these e-books into action, but have it in mind that if they buy a certain e-book, they will learn a life-altering secret. When they are finished reading the book (if they bother to read it), they don't put it into action because they realize that it takes more work than they had perceived. A month later, they are back to searching the internet for the same thing as before– a magic formula to succeed in an aspect of life, such as money, looks, or health. They gobble up these e-books like there is no tomorrow... at least the ones that have good advertising. The sellers of most of these e-books rarely reveal anything you shouldn't already know. The sellers are well aware that you probably already know what they have to say. They offer money back guarantees because they know that more than seventy-five per cent of people will put the e-book on the back burner, forgetting to send in for a refund, thus allowing the company to profit.

HOPE is therefore the first of the five aspects that I ALWAYS use to make a website that sells. You can give people hope in multiple ways, with many different products, but I find it best with informational products, since you can get away with promising almost anything and then delivering less. Tell potential customers what they yearn to hear. Hope, however, can also apply to physical products such as a credit card. "Get your credit card today and re-build your credit quicker". You may also see

"Order the super computer today and do things on a computer you never dreamed that you could do." This is not enough to convince you to enroll in the credit card or buy the computer, but hope exists.

2. Try to instill a Feeling of Urgency

Another aspect of a successful website that will definitely sell is if you manage to instill a feeling of **URGENCY**. You have probably seen various kinds of products and services put up on sale that say, "order by 12.00 a.m tonight and you will be sure to get a twenty dollar discount or buy now and receive this".

I promise you that if you go back to that very page on the next day, there are high chances that it will convey the same message. Purchasers usually consider and are quite aware of that, but do not want to take such a big risk, just in case the discount is not available the following day! It is very probable that being impulsive purchasers, they will never take the chance on losing out on such a great offer!

I would advise that instead of writing a "by 12.00 a.m" html script that can be very effortlessly noticed to be unreal by most people who are net savvy, you should attempt to make a real and believable deadline of the very last day of any month or something like two weeks from a current date, and try to hard code it into the website. Then, once that deadline gets over, you can try making some new deadline. One more intelligent strategy can be by saying only the next fifty members will be accepted, and then implement an image of 50 to get crossed out, and a numerical figure such as forty-two positioned beside it, being sure to update and leave the number at forty-two.

3. Try to look like a Figure of Authority

Another aspect of a successful site that will definitely be popular is to look like a figure of **AUTHORITY**. Regardless of what you are trying to sell, you have to look like a professional on the topic of discussion. Keep in mind that appearance is vital.

You may ask yourself that why would you want to purchase a gambling e-book from someone who provides proof that he or she actually won two hundred dollars at a particular card game at one instance?

As a matter of fact, you want an e-book from someone who won eight million dollars at gambling! One successful method of marketing is to seem as an authority who is impartial. If you manage to appear as a person who is only trying to provide some assistance, and is not actually benefitting from the purchase of various products and services mentioned on your website, then you are one more stage closer to your goal. People usually tend to heed the guidance of independent and expert reviewers who provide their frank opinions of products or services.

There is no need for them to find out that you receive any kind of commission for such sales.

4. Try to Appear Impartial

The fourth feature aspect of a successful site that can become popular is to seem as an impartial third party. Review products in such a manner as though you want to aid people in making decisions, but do not allow it to be guessed that you are somewhat affiliated or obligated to them. Take a look at the sales letter demonstrating this technique below.

5. Give importance to Fear

Another characteristic of a successfully selling website is by instilling a FEAR. You should create some kind of fear in the minds of your visitors and influence them in believing that they will face serious consequences in the future if they consume a similar product or service other than yours, or if they simply do not purchase yours right away...How? Something along the lines of: "- How to become wealthy instantly Scams Exposed..."

Then you can write an elaborate article on numerous occurrences of become wealthy instantly fraud, being careful not to take names. Avoid specifics when discussing scams, as you want to avoid the legal trouble that it may bring.

After you have written your article, you can consider saying that during your entire in-depth research required for the exposé write up, you happened to locate a few money-making strategies with which numerous visitors were quite satisfied every time. You can say that you had a discussion with one of the owners and they were forthright and honest.

Thus, you have now managed to make a good impression. Now you can push your visitors to the websites for which you are surely going to receive the highest amount of commission from.

6. Try to be as UNUSUAL as possible (optional-since it should be used for generating sales of your own services and products)

If you have decided to sell your own service or product, then you must be careful since it will not be possible for you to apply the aspects of fear or scam.

You may have to rely on urgency and authority. You also require implementing the UNUSUAL aspect. Try reverse psychology. Maybe they should not purchase your service or product. It's true —you must influence them NOT to consume your service or product unless they have already attempted using the services and products of your competitors' and become dissatisfied with them. You will be very sure beforehand that they are bound to be so. Tell them to go a little back and refer to your homepage. Remind them that you told them several times that they should NOT buy this e-book until your potential consumers actually become fed up of all the other various programs. Maybe the service or product of your company is somewhat inferior and more expensive. The whimsical approach of telling or convincing people to avoid the product or service of your company will definitely work. If you manage to convince them that you really want them to try out other products and services other than yours, that you are sure will disappoint them, will naturally earn you a sense or loyalty, since you appear to be interested in the customer's benefit more than generating any form of sales.

FINAL PRODUCT:

Now, let us put all five aspects (remember, the sixth is optional) into a small sample sales letter which, according to aspect four, shouldn't really look like a sales letter. Let's use the get rich quick subject again, as it's a hugely popular subject on the internet (see next page).

Creating Killer Copy

Creating a successful sales letter is a key aspect to determine whether your business will succeed or fail.

General Tips

Do not rely solely on all capital letters in the text of your message. It will slow the average reader down up to thirty per cent and is very annoying, as it signals shouting. Only use capital letters when you want to emphasize a point, but remember that there are other ways to demonstrate emphasis, such as using bold text.

Have an enticing sales letter or sales message.

Make it interactive or else use words that excite the reader to prevent drowsiness from boredom caused by reading a sterile text.

- Use small words and short sentences or phrases. People don't want to read a long, difficult copy of more than a few pages.

- Make sure that the entire copy flows logically allowing one point to flow naturally to the next and making the offer easy to follow. Describe who you are to the prospective customer. Explain the benefits. Be clear, concise, and proactive about asking for the order. Ask yourself, "Is everything about how the order works explained in detail so that the customer feels comfortable? If they have any questions, do I ask them to contact me and provide my contact information?"

- Get testimonials and publish them. It is easy to e-mail your past customers asking them to rate your service or product. By posting these comments in your sales message it creates credibility for you and your business. There are many ways to get testimonials, but one of the easiest ways is to offer your product free to a few people "in exchange" for their comments on it. Explain that their testimonial could be used in your national advertising campaign, or in magazine or TV ads (assuming that you will grow big enough to advertise in these mediums).

- Write your sales letter as though you were talking **TO** somebody – a friend - not **AT** them. Be informal in language and keep it uncomplicated in understandable. It is next to impossible to close a sale unless the customer feels as though he or she is getting personal attention. Avoid too many large words and difficult concepts. Once you are done with the letter, read it out loud and ask yourself, "Does this sound like me when I am talking?"

- *The way that you write shows who you are.* Make sure that all of your information is clear, concise, effective, and error-free. Poor spelling is unprofessional and a poor reflection. Vague writing style will not only cost you sales, but also costs you extra time answering questions that should have become clear the first time.

- *"Saying something is free has a lot of weight behind it.* Avoid advertising "free samples" if you expect the user to pay for anything, including return postage. The minute you abuse this word is the minute you lost your respect and sales. Free means "no cost to consumer".

- Discuss the benefits of your products before features. For example, don't say "this xxxx has a, b, c, d....instead say the xxxx will save you time and money because it has a, b, and c features. Define the ultimate benefits that your clients want by putting them into terms they can easily understand (i.e. "laymen's" terms, no big words or difficult sentence structures).

Your potential customers do not care if your product has "super-strength" or if it will last longer, look better, or for what it is designed, or every feature it has... what they care about is what it will do for them (i.e. benefits, benefits, benefits!). Show them how your product is a solution to their problem. By offering benefits instead of features you are creating a higher perceived value, which translates into more sales.

The real question at hand is "how to get these benefits?" It's simple. List your product or service's features on a piece of paper. On another sheet of paper list all the benefits affiliated with each feature. If you can't think of a benefit for a feature, don't even bother listing that feature in your sales literature.

When you create your sales letter, briefly list the features and then give a detailed description of the benefits each feature provides.

Try to place yourself in the position of the buyer and understand what they want, then show them how to fulfill that need. It is harder to sell benefit or a feature. Instead, aim to sell an answer. Your marketing should focus on a few problems, and offer your product or service as the perfect solution.

Don't say anything behind which you are not comfortable standing. For example, saying "We are the best and we are cheaper than everyone else" is too strong, and poorly written. It makes you look like a cheap, small business. Saying "Serving you with quality and low prices" promises or conveys a benefit to the reader. Also it uses the word "you" and the promise is not overstated (not too hyped).

Some words have power to **turn prospects on** and encourage their purchase. Some examples of words that make people want to read on are:

Free	Sale	Discover	Natural
Love	Now	Introduce	Fast
Safe	Value	Easy	Precious
New	Fun	Your	Secret
Benefits	Save	Proven	Solution
Right	Gain	Penetrate	Magic
You	Money	Suddenly	Comfortable
Alternative	Happy	Proud	Advice
Healthy	Security	How to	Guarantee

A partial list of words to avoid since they may make people want to stop reading is:

Buy	Failure	Cost	Loss
Difficult	Decision	Sell	Hard
Death	Fail	Taxes	Contract
Obligation	Bad	Liability	Wrong
Deal	Worry		

Always transfer ownership in your sales letters to make them more personal by using "you" and "your". Say "You will learn...," not "the book has..." or "your widget will be delivered in five days", not "the widget will be delivered in five days." Count the number of "yous" and "yours" in your sales material. You should have at least twice as many "yous" and "yours" as "Is", "wes", "mes", "ours" or the company's name.

- **"Fear of loss" and "desire of gain" is something that needs to be in all sales material.** Being afraid to lose is by far more powerful. You are risking the loss of this benefit if you don't buy now. The capital that you gain or save if you buy the product is based on desire, not fear. This desire should still be considered a valuable sales tool.

- **Be sure to have a "no questions asked, money back guarantee".** Be specific, explaining each detail and using the guarantee as a condition of doing business. If you have a good product you will not have a lot of returns.

- **Make sure that you are clear about the ordering process and be precise when stating what they will receive.** Have a truly dynamite reason for someone to respond to the sales letter. Offer a bonus or discount if they order now.

- **Make sure that you have multiple ways of ordering** including directly online, 800 number(s), fax, and/or mail.

- **You want a relationship starting from the beginning.** Don't be afraid to tell a story so that the prospect feels like they know you or your business. For example, with two one-hour photo stores, one store charges three dollars more for processing. When one of the customers asked "why," the more expensive store gave him a tour of their facilities, pointed out their $80,000 piece of machinery and explained how they were specially trained to operate that machinery. He then pointed out their special print and chemical recycling program (environmentally friendly), and their policy of redoing prints at their own expense if the photos weren't up to their demanding standards...

For those who might be saying now that they are too old, that the internet is for the youth, the next generation, YOU'RE WRONG!! There is no limit as to who is capable. Your great grand pappy Earl can do it. Your seven year old child can do it (though make sure he knows to ask his parents- there is a lot of danger out there).

Time to find a new way (Ultimate internet strategy)

It is hard to envision, working from home

It is hard to enlighten, people that feel alone

It's time for change, time to tell the people

Time to think fresh, time to stop being feeble

There are opportunities, to make money from home

There are ways to market, our companies that set the tone

The world is in turmoil, and this has affected our economy

The world is in disarray, and put our future in jeopardy

Chorus

It's time to tell the message, to all our pupils

It's time to spread the message, like the disciples

Time to teach the new ways that will secure our future

Time to teach the new methods to the young and mature.

Affiliate programs and quality, should be taught in our schools

Killer sales copy and marketing will stop us looking like fools

Sincere passion and domains will help us avoid economic pain,

With no work or money, sooner or later you will go insane,

You need to be patient and persistent, you must never give in

Through the bad times and hard times, to quit would be a sin

It's just a question of sticking with it, and trying your best

To help you persevere and get through it, think of it as test

Chorus

It's time to tell the message, to all our pupils

It's time to spread the message, like the disciples

Time to teach the new ways that will secure our future

Time to teach the new methods, to the young and mature

University students should be well versed, in the ways of the web,

University students should know all there is, in the ways to get ahead,

For the good times will only roll, if our children know all there is,

About using the web for working from home, and doing the biz,

The old business methods are not as good, as they used to be,

The old business ways have to move over, it is plain to see,

Overheads, such as rental costs, do not need to be considered,

If the internet home market, is used and properly configured.

Chorus

It's time to tell the message, to all our pupils

It's time to spread the message, like the disciples

Time to teach the new ways that will secure our future

Time to teach the new methods, to the young and mature

1.B Affiliate Programs

In marketing your own product, one way to raise your sales exponentially is an affiliate program.

Affiliate programs allow you to bring in an unknown number of individuals to sell products for you. The key to gaining affiliates is to offer a good commission on a per sale basis. The higher the commission, the more affiliates you will have.

There are scores of affiliate programs available on the Internet and elsewhere. To succeed, you must sell your affiliate program the same way that you need to sell your product. The affiliate letter should mimic a sales letter. You have to convince visitors to join your affiliate program. One surefire way to do this is by packing your affiliate sales letter with benefits. Tell them what your program will do for them, how much commission they will receive and keep the sign-up process simple.

You can offer a seventy-five per cent commission for affiliates. That's the maximum commission allowed by Clickbank, and you will attract more affiliates that way. Some companies entice me to join their affiliate program by offering me an additional two or three dollars per sale, on top of the seventy-five per cent commission through Clickbank. I get these bonuses via PayPal at the end of each month.

You might want to consider offering this type of bonus to your super affiliates also. If they are able to bring hundreds or even thousands of sales to your site every month, then offering them a Paypal bonus per sale is a smart move, as it will encourage them to promote your site and continue to do so over all of the other similar sites. You might make fewer sales dollars yourself, but if the volume is high, it will be well worth it. At the end of the month, add up the number of sales, less refunds from your super affiliates, and send them the Paypal bonus.

You should have some banners created for your site, and put them on your affiliate page so your affiliates can use them to send people your way.

Another way to find super affiliates to promote your website is to go to Google and type in the name of the product you "emulated" and see what hits come up that promote that product. *Ask for help.* . Request that webmasters take your site for a test drive. Be persistent, friendly, and confident when you tell them that they will earn more with your program. Just copy and paste the same e-mail to each webmaster. Let them know that you have a lower refund percentage. You can even pay someone you know a few dollars to e-mail people for you. I do that, since I don't have the time or inclination to send out e-mail!

One Tier Compared to Two Tier

The affiliate programs of one tier essentially pay commissions only on a single level. Such an affiliate thus makes commission a basis of per sale. For instance, if you make an offer of a commission of thirty percent to your affiliates and your product manages to sell for an amount of $39.99, then for every sale that your affiliate incurs, they will be receiving a commission of $12.

Similarly, the affiliate programs of two tier are called so since they are supposed to pay commissions specifically on two distinct levels. The affiliates receive a commission for every sale that they make and also for every sale that their recruits incur. These two tier affiliate programs divide their commissions conveniently over two levels. Thus, if you happen to provide your affiliates an entire 30% commission for every sale, you will be expected to give a 20% commission on their sales of the first level and an extra 10% commission for the sales of the second level. Also, if your affiliate makes a sale of $39.99, they would rightfully receive a commission of $8. If any one of the recruits of your affiliates make a sale, then they would receive an extra commission of $4.

How to increase Affiliate Sales

You are supposed to know your product better than anyone else. You should provide your affiliates with things that will benefit and help them. These may include sample advertisements and banners.

If you wish to increase your sales even further, then you must target your e-book towards a particular group or audience and encourage its free distribution and circulation. This electronic book should comprise essential information and data and must also be usable as a sales tool specifically for your product. It will be sensible to customize a copy of your electronic book for every affiliate and permit them to freely distribute them. You can opt for the customization of such e-books all by yourself or buy an e-book compiler to assist you in this process. These compilers typically allow your affiliates to customize your electronic books completely on their own. However, you should know there are certain compliers that do not allow any form of customization.

To ensure better encouragement of your affiliates, you can consider creating an opt-in list that will enable them in the subscription and reception of the latest and most updated methods of promotion, articles and sales letters. This will help in the assessment of their capability to generate more sales. Apart from increasing sales, this will also enable you to be in constant contact with all your affiliates and you can introduce brand new products if you wish to.

How to Set Up Your Own Affiliate Program

Once you get started with your affiliate program, you will basically have two broad options. These generally include the buying of an affiliate program of software or the use of a third party. If you decide to actually purchase the software, then you must know how it can help you. Such software generally enables you to track and closely follow affiliate sales. It can also assist affiliates have a look at their statistics.

A minor drawback of this option is that it is relatively more time consuming. This is due to the fact that you are required to run your affiliate program on your own. Thus, you become completely responsible in terms of accepting payments or even sending out checks for commission. Nevertheless, it definitely helps you to be in proper control.

The second option involves the use of a third party company that specializes in affiliate tracking. Such companies are useful in tracking your affiliate sales. They also assist your affiliates to have a look at their statistics. They will even send out checks for commission on your behalf. Thus you will be saved on a lot of time and effort.

Companies of Affiliate Tracking

ClickBank- this company typically permits you to receive credit cards. They will also undertake the running of your affiliate program. More than 60,000 affiliates are associated in this company and they may consider selling products for you.

ClickBank also enables web sales in paying commissions for sales automatically. Thus, this is very similar to a direct form of payment. They will also do a host of activities for your benefit. These include the billing of your customers, paying of commission to your affiliates and even paying you. You will simply need to pay a one-time activation fee of $49.99. Then onwards you will be expected to pay $1 and a ½% fee for every sale. They will not charge you any fees on a monthly basis.

Click Trade- is another reputed company for affiliate tracking that can assist you in creating your own and distinct affiliate program and even provide for others to send you customers who pay. You will be able to catch the attention of new potential customers by getting featured on several affiliate sites. This company has more than 120,000 affiliates who are lined up from before for participating and being associated with your program of affiliation.

The Decision is Yours

You must take your time in making the best decision. You should select the best option for affiliating your business. If you are in the initial setting up stage of your business, then you can consider using any of the third party companies of affiliates. This is usually more convenient and simple. You can also be rest assured that all your work will be done for you. In this way, you can focus better on sales as well as development.

ClickBank: How you can create as well as sell a particular product on Clickbank and how you can become an affiliate of other merchants of ClickBank.

There are many internet users around the world who wish to know about the best ten methods that can improve their life. These people are also eager to spend a lot of money on e-books that will be able to explain these things to them very clearly. This is the reason why ClickBank happens to be such an excellent affiliate network. Their main focus is completely on products that are non-material. This signifies and includes all matter or data that you can possibly send via e-mail or even download as an electronic book.

What is the best way to create information products?

The best way to get it done and done right is to do it yourself. If you become lazy and subcontract the work to somebody else to write, what kind of e-book are you going to sell? Frankly, I would strongly recommend doing something that has always been really overdone. This is true and I'm not joking. You must have realized that discussions on quitting smoking, acne loss or even or weight loss have sold for many decades and continues to do so even now. Hence, you should not expect things to be any different now! As far as online information products go, ClickBank is the number one affiliate network. They have a vast network of affiliates who funnel customers directly to you.

You can also sign up as an affiliate of other products on ClickBank. Be sure that your website reviews some of the products available on Clickbank. Every time you send a paying customer, there is an opportunity for a commission of up to seventy-five per cent. It is really easy to choose to whom you want to link. Next to each product in the ClickBank Marketplace (Click on "promote products" on ClickBank's homepage) they tell you the exact percentage commission that gets paid out for the product. This makes it easy to browse through the sea of options, and find a plan that makes you money.

1.C Pay Per Click

If you want website traffic right away, you're going to need advertisements that bring visitors to your website. The best way to get quick results is with a Pay per Click (PPC) search engine like Google, Yahoo, MSN, MIVA or a dozen or so smaller search engines up with which are worth signing. For those who have not grasped it yet, PPC means you pay only when someone clicks on your ad. It's an established system of advertising system that ensures that you get targeted traffic on your site. PPC search engines are a good tool for advertising since they allow you to commit a fixed amount of money for a certain campaign. It can be one hundred or $100,000—it doesn't matter. You get the option of how much you want to spend each time someone clicks on your promo every time that they search for a specific keyword. For instance, if you are selling something like headphones, then a standard cost per click or CPC would be somewhere around two bucks or so. If this turns into a sale of twenty dollars or so, then there's no arguing that it's truly worth it. Most of the PPC search engines possess interfaces thus enabling you to make an input of your keyword or key phrase terms and gauge an estimated expenditure of getting your ad run for specific keywords or key phrases. Let us assume that all other PPC advertisements that are placing their bids on "headphones" obtain 1000 click per day. At a rate of two bucks for every click, it can really become substantial very rapidly. This is where PPC campaigns can get kind of pricy. It is possible that you could spend thousands of dollars a day simply on advertising, though it is always possible to set a cap on how much you want to spend, in order to avoid getting burned.

Have individual, specialized terms. Some keywords are less expensive, or less searched and can even have higher conversion rates than the more searched keywords. The best part about PPC search engines is that you can turn around your campaign every day. If you have words that don't convert, or are too expensive, the words can be filed and replaced with a new set.

You might have some idea that there are a handful of good and reliable PPC search engines that are used by internet surfers around the world. These are available in the form of websites where you are supposed to bid an amount that you are ready to pay for every visitor to get sent to your own website for a specific keyword. If you plan to sell books, you can bid up to an upper limit of 25cents to get your advertisement appear on these particular websites whenever any online surfer looks for some other book that you are already selling.

The Most Popular ones are:

Google –AdWords and AdSense

Yahoo (earlier Overture)

And Miva (earlier it was Espotting and Findwhat)

Here it becomes essential to point out that Google basically has two main services of advertising – these are AdWords and AdSense

AdWords is primarily meant and suited for those advertisers who wish to direct traffic only from Google and from its partners as well.

AdSense, on the other hand, is best suited for publishers. These include people who have their own websites, and also want to get affiliated to Google as a partner. This is where such advertisements appear.

Google basically displays advertisements on your website. These are those advertisements that the advertisers of AdWords pay for.

Google divides its profits with all the publishers of AdSense. Although Google chooses not to divulge the exact percentage, most experts are of the opinion that it is somewhere around 50%.

Google AdWords

Google AdWords allows you only a limited amount of text words on your AdWords ads, so you have to make each one count. Remember that individuality is what makes us unique.

The best method to do this that I know of is still fear, or causing someone to be almost disturbed by the uniqueness, absurdity or humour of your ad.

If you can convince people that buying your competitor's product will wind up in some sort of disappointment or financial loss, you will stand out. There is never a need to identify names. Using humour or quirky statements draws attention as well.

Advertisements similar to those shown below should raise your CTR (click through rate). If you have a higher CTR than your competitors, you probably end up paying less per click and having higher place in the sponsored ad results.

Google, it is well-known, favors ads. These ads are those that consistently have a high CTR.

There is no way to make money before getting traffic to your website, and one of the best ways I've found is advertising your website through Google Adwords. This is the biggest PPC (pay per click) program on the web so it is obvious that you should take advantage of this opportunity to drive up traffic.

To set up an account with Google AdWords accounts go to adwords.google.com.

There are a few things you have to know about Ad words because using this program is nothing like putting up a banner.

There is solely text without images. You have a minute amount of space to write your advertisement. Usually, it is a headline followed by two lines and your website's URL. That's all.

It could be that you are questioning the effectiveness. You have no reason for questions. Why not? In AdWords, only relevant ads are returned when they're relevant to the content on the remainder of the webpage that the potential consumer visits. They also show up on search engine results pages when people input keywords that relate to your ad. (The "sponsored listings" found on the right of the results pages). AdWords advertisers succeed because their ads are seen only by those actively seeking information about the product or service.

The third thing you need to know is this: as an AdWords advertiser, you get to choose for which keywords you want your ad to show. You are going to have to pay more for the terms that get a lot of traffic, because they're much more competitive.

If your potential client Googles "video games," and you've chosen "video games" as a trigger keyword phrase, then your ad will be a "sponsored link" on the right side of Google's search results page. Should your campaign be really good, you might even make it to the shaded blue box above the results page.

Of note here is the example "video games" is a highly competitive term, increasing the expense per click, but also lowering the visibility. Many sponsored links get relegated to a second page. The moment people start clicking on it, though, you'll begin to move up the rankings toward the top position, and traffic will start pouring in.

Up to then, you might want to consider bidding on terms that are not as competitive, so that you show up as one of the first sponsored links when a visitor does search for that term. These terms also cost less per click, and if you bid for many, you can get visitors from all over the world.

Along with this, you can choose to have your site show up on Google partners' sites, like America Online, EarthLink, AskJeeves and many others. There's also the choice for your ads to show up on any websites that are relevant to what you're advertising. You can even have your ads show up on Google's webmail service, Gmail, when users send e-mails that include relevant content.

Google claims that its AdWords program reaches out to eighty per cent of Internet users — I don't doubt it. They are everywhere. If you want to avoid having your ads all over the Google network, you have the option to remove yourself from any partner sites, Gmail or anything else. Should people make return visits to one site and click your ads, and not buy anything, you should remove those ads. You wouldn't want to pay with no return profits. Be sure to watch your AdWords conversion rates.

1.D E-mails

Efficient use of e-mail is critical because you can expect to receive fifty or one hundred   e-mail messages every day when your business is up and running. This section covers many different aspects of e-mail management to conduct your business with ease.

Don't overlook some of the simpler things, since they can be very important for your success. An example of what I mean can be found in the use of an **"electronic signature"**.

Most of you will know about signatures, but for those who don't...you should because it's critical for any campaign forum and newsgroup posting success. "Sig" file (as it is referred to) is a three to six line "footer" at the bottom of all your e-mail messages and all newsgroup postings.

A signature is the information displayed at the bottom of your e-mail message. It tells the person you're writing to, who you are and how to get a hold of you. It is a universally accepted way of advertising your company, product or service.

You can even include your autoresponder address, 1-800 number or office telephone in the signature.

It is critical to at least include the URL, e-mail address, and a slogan or description of what you have to offer (including some kind of benefit to the reader for contacting you).

Many people don't want phone calls but don't deny a potential customer the opportunity to talk to you for personal service. Also mention your physical address in your e-mail if there is room, in order to give your business credibility (you are not just an anonymous e-mail address and website).

Try to limit your signature to six lines - more than that is not only considered bad etiquette, but many of the mailing lists you post to will cut it off after six lines.

Another way to approach signatures (especially when it comes to newsgroup, forum, or mailing list postings) is to make your message noticeable by placing text around it. You can do this by creating "ASCII text art" (sometimes called line art) or a border around your signature.

Autoresponder

An **autoresponder**, also called a Mailbot or Infobot, is basically a small program that will get a service provider to automatically send a document (a simple e-mail or any kind of file) to any user who sends a request to its e-mail address.

Autoresponders are an absolute necessity for doing business on the Internet. They are just one of the things you need in order to make your business fully automated. The problem is, most people either misuse them or do not use them to their fullest potential.

I am sure that most of you are at least somewhat familiar with autoresponders, but for those that are not, let me quickly run over some basics.

Not all autoresponders are equal, and simply shopping for the lowest price is not the best way to proceed.

Here are a few considerations when shopping for an autoresponder service:

- You must have personal control over your autoresponder documents. In other words, you should have the ability to upload new autoresponder documents anytime you want (via FTP... File Transfer Protocol). This allows you to change your documents twenty-four hours a day, seven days a week, instantaneously.
- The autoresponder must be user friendly. Some services require you to specify an exact "subject" or "body" message in order to retrieve the document you want. Although these work, they are difficult for the user to understand and customers must follow instructions EXACTLY or they will get nothing and you have a chance of losing the sale.

For simplicity's sake, use an autoresponder that sends a specific message back to the requester regardless of what is in the subject or body of the e-mail message that was sent. In other words, you don't have to explain how to retrieve a document because ANY (even a blank message) e-mail to that address will trigger a response. This type of autoresponder requires you to have a separate e-mail address for every document you want your customer to retrieve.

As an example, with separate autoresponder addresses, if your customer wanted information on your product X, they would just send any e-mail to x@xyz.com and for information on product Y, just send any e-mail to y@xyz.com.

With "non-user friendly" autoresponders, one e-mail address can control more than one document. For example, to get info on product X, they would have to send an e-mail to product@xyz.com with the word "product x" typed in the SUBJECT heading. If they wanted to get info on product Y, they would have to send an e-mail to product@xyz.com with the word "product y" typed in the SUBJECT heading. If these exact instructions are not followed, the potential client will get nothing. In other words, if they typed "product x" in the BODY of the message, (instead of the SUBJECT heading) or made a typo like "productx" (no space), or any other kind of mistake, they will get nothing.

You can't imagine the number of people who e-mail you saying your autoresponder does not work and upon investigation the error is on their part in one way or another. With separate e-mail autoresponders, they just send an e-mail to the address (no matter what is in the e-mail) and the autoresponder sends back the requested document.

Most autoresponders will only send up to 32K of information. You don't want one of these (it may do for now, but when you grow and try new ideas, it may cause you problems, and you want to be prepared for the future. It will be easier now than switching later). Make sure your autoresponder has the capability of sending any size e-mail and attachment so that you can send graphics, software, and detailed assistance manuals for your product or service, et cetera.

Be sure you know how fast your server will set up additional autoresponders if you need them. For example, if you are testing an ad, a request to your autoresponder xyz@domain.com may indicate a response to your ad at site #1, while a request to abc@domain.com may indicate a response to your ad at site #2. You may need additional autoresponders quickly in order to trace advertisements, so your ISP will have to set these up quickly or give you access to set them up yourself.

Will the autoresponder capture and log every e-mail address that requests a response? This is a critically important question because if you have a list of e-mail addresses you will be able to follow up on all of your customer leads. Another consideration is whether these logs show the time and date of the request so that you can track activity as well. Do not get an autoresponder that does not have these features!

Make sure the ISP's autoresponder software will allow you to download the autoresponder log (I download mine every twenty-one to thirty days) and rebuild a new log automatically so you don't wind up with duplicates. This allows you to strip out e-mail addresses from each log and correspond with the potential customers again.

On the "down" side, beware of autoresponders that:

- charge high set up fees (i.e.: twenty-five to seventy-five dollars is unacceptable),
- charge more than ten dollars per autoresponder per month,
- charge a "per hit" charge each time a document is requested,
- Require you to submit your document to the ISP for uploading instead of giving you the ability to control the upload and change the document yourself.
- Life time membership for a one-time fee. Most of them do not give you good service as they have already collected your fees.

Most people use autoresponders for sending out free articles, sales letters, et cetera. They post ads in newsgroups, discussion lists, forums and classified ads, asking people to e-mail their autoresponder for more information. This is great and will make you money... but it is also a limited way of thinking. I will show you how to really use autoresponders in ways that almost nobody else does. Autoresponders are designed to handle large volumes of requests for certain information, by sending it out at specified intervals. This allows you to follow up with your customers on time, every time, without bogging you down in e-mails. It is all done automatically by the autoresponder.

There will be examples throughout different sections of unique autoresponder techniques that will skyrocket your sales.

We will not discuss those here as they belong in a later section. Instead of me preaching to you about the different ways of using autoresponders, let me give you some examples of how I use them myself to show you how powerful they can be if used properly. You will get ideas on how they can save you a mountain of time, stress and increase your sales without much work. Apply the use of autoresponders to your business by copying my techniques.

Bulk e-mail can be used for many things. It can be a mass mailing to your clientele list, newsletter list, opt-in list or it can be unsolicited e-mail (which has earned it the reputation of being "spam"). We will be talking a lot about the different kinds of bulk e-mail throughout this section.

There are as many good ways to use bulk e-mail as there are bad. This type of e-mail is usually used to denote or signify spam. It should be made clear that these are not the same things. Bulk e-mail essentially refers to a group of individuals. On the other hand, spam entails the sending of mass quantity of mails electronically to random internet users with whom the sender has no relationship with at all.

Please understand the differences, as we will be discussing the various types of bulk e-mail in this section... from opt-in to spam.

I will also be using the word "bulk e-mail" and will refer to people as "bulk e-mailers" throughout this section. Please note that I am, most of the time (until near the end of this section), not referring to spam, but to sending mass e-mail (a.k.a. bulk e-mail) to a list of people...that could include leads, newsletter lists, customers, opt-in lists, follow ups on autoresponder and others. All of these are completely ethical without being controversial at the same time. If I am referring to spam in a sentence, I will call it by its name "spam", not "bulk e-mail".

On that note, there will always be extremely opinionated people who will go overboard to fight spamming of any kind... and there will also be others who will do anything to fight for its legitimacy. Be prepared to meet both of those types of people (and lots of others in between). Everyone has his or her own opinion about spamming.

In the past, some people have gotten the impression that I endorse spam. So I want to make a few statements as to why that is simply not correct and why we discuss spam in the e-book. You see, my job in this e-book is to show you all the marketing techniques being used!

It becomes very vital to know what exactly to look for so that you can supersede your competitors. You must also be aware of the techniques that will help you in making money and the techniques that should be strictly avoided. You will find innumerable promotional techniques and methods that are widely available. You can make a decision by choosing one that best meets your requirements.

Here is my thought... if I don't tell you about spam... what it is, how it is done, and the pros and cons of it, you will just surf the net to find info. You will then most likely find some bulk e-

43

mail / spamming website that will build it up to be the "be-all and end-all" of marketing online… and pitch you on how it will make you rich. You will end up spamming millions of people (or at least trying to), getting yourself in a lot of hot water, and not making a dime. In this section I will tell you the truth about bulk e-mail (different kinds like opt-in and unsolicited). I will tell you some things you don't want to hear and others that you do… you can then make your decision on what you want to do and not base it on someone else's false promises or figures.

Newsletters

There are two main types of newsletters; those that are free and those that are not.

Newsletters are very effective for increasing sales, both now and long term.

You must have free subscriptions to newsletters available on your website and in print. Subscription instructions for your free newsletter should not only be at your website in very high traffic areas, but also in the signature files on all your e-mails and newsgroup/forum and mailing list postings.

Think about this. People who subscribe to your newsletter will become very loyal customers if you show them that you are honest, credible, and most of all… you really do know what you are talking about.

They will not only buy what you are offering now, they will also buy entirely different products that you offer in the future because you will already have built a rapport with them.

Now normally, this would be considered to be a "no-no" as you always want to target your market… but this is the exception to the rule. I only offer the course to Car Secrets book purchasers because I have built a rapport with them, they believe in me, and know that I will not cheat them. At the time I offer them the course, I really have nothing else to backend to them…so I have nothing to lose.

You may be thinking "I don't have a newsletter, nor do I want one". Let me tell you, you may not have one now, but you will want one in the future because it will bring in tons of cash. Let me give you some reasons for starting a free newsletter.

Think about the following scenario:

A potential client surfing the web for information on accounting stumbles on your website (and you happen to be selling a particular package of accounting software). Remember, they are searching through scores of websites and just happen to hit yours. If you don't grab them the first few seconds, they will simply click a button on their browser and move to the next website…YOU WILL NEVER SEE THIS CUSTOMER AGAIN, NOR WILL YOU EVER HAVE THE CHANCE TO SELL THEM ANYTHING.

Now imagine a different scenario:

This person surfs and reaches your website and sees the offer of a free monthly newsletter on tax tips and accounting software shortcuts and innovations. They sign up for your newsletter, which retains the person's interest in your website a little longer and gets them interacting with it. They are more tempted now to explore it even further. Even if the person decides to move on to the next site, you have their e-mail address and will be able to send them your monthly newsletter, giving you the chance to sell your product or service every month.

I am not saying your monthly newsletter should be a sales letter every month, it should not! You should have informative tips and updates as promised… but it doesn't hurt to "plug" your product or service on the last couple of lines at the end of every issue.

The newsletter will give you the chance to offer special promotional pricing to "subscribers only", updates, announcements of new products/services, offer something extra free of charge with their purchase – whatever it takes to get them to buy.

The subscriber base is more than a random sampling of people. It is a specific list of potential clients with whom you have built credibility and who feel comfortable with you. When it comes to having a potential customer, it can't get any better than this — that is why I highly recommend you start a newsletter.

You will have to choose a topic for the newsletter.

It could be something related to the product you sell or you are an expert on or have "insider" knowledge about.

It could be informative articles you have gathered, tips or interesting sites to visit.

It could be about industry news and updates, new product announcements, and most importantly what is new on your site are also items you might include.

You see, you can have great information in a newsletter even if you are not an expert on the subject. Of course it should always include a short, low key blurb about one of your products or services to make it easy for your potential customers to become your customers.

There are a few different ways of running newsletters. A very basic way can be with the help of really special software present on anyone's server that is specifically devised for discussion lists as well as for newsletters (i.e. some of the more popular stuff is Listserve, Majordomo, or customer built list management software like Lyris). Your ISP can require you to pay a monthly fee based on the size of your membership. If you have a newsletter subscriber base of 2,000 or more people (which is very easy to get), you can expect a one hundred dollar set-up fee and fifty dollar or more a month just to maintain the list. Once the subscriber base of your newsletters expands, you will have to pay a greater amount every month (this can be as substantial as $500 per month if your list increases considerably).

If your ISP does not offer Listserve or Majordomo newsletter capabilities, you can go to http://www.listserve.com for this service or find another provider by typing in the keywords "listserve service" or "majordomo service" in any of the major search engines.

The next way a newsletter can be used is for a program such as Mailloop. When you purchase it, it is free to run your newsletter, no matter how large. With Mailloop you can do everything yourself or have someone else do so, even from elsewhere. Someone else will be able to run everything in the newsletter with a login name and password from any computer, anywhere in the world

It is a complete program, allowing you your freedom. It subscribes, unsubscribes, and sends out your monthly newsletter. This is probably the most effective way (especially as you stop to think about everything that Mailloop does with e-mail and newsgroups)! It also lets you to make alterations to your newsletter list and fulfill related functions off-line, instead of having to be connected to the Internet (Mailloop is hosted on your PC, not the ISP's server).

You can have as many newsletters as you desire. For example, you could:

- Create a free newsletter (promoted on your website, sig file, and in your advertisements) that updating subscribers on alterations to your site... or with compelling articles or free information in each issue.

- Have an "additional" bonus newsletter that gets sent to those having already bought your goods or services, giving them incentives such as deals or information on your industry.

- ● Have a newsletter your customer base pays for before they can subscribe.

There are many people who charge upward of two hundred dollars per year for a subscription to their newsletter. If the information you offer is valuable and cannot be found anywhere else for free, people will pay you for it.

On this note, I must say there are a lot of people who make thousands of dollars selling their newsletters and it is not uncommon to find a newsletter author making over $100,000. Again, the principle being, if you truly have something of value to offer, people are willing to pay for it.

Think about what you are really good at, and how you can transform that knowledge into a newsletter. You can easily charge thirty dollars or more per year for this information.

If your information will make someone else's life more pleasant or make them more money, it would not be uncommon to charge one hundred and fifty dollars or more for your information. I know of electronic newsletters on stock market predictions that cost nine hundred fifty dollars or more per year. If the publisher only gets five hundred subscribers, after all of their expenses, they are making $400,000 a year from just one newsletter!

A personal client of mine for whom I designed a full internet marketing and promotions strategy for, sells a newsletter online for two hundred seventy-seven dollars (it is about stock market investing). He has about five hundred subscribers and is gaining more every day.

Do the math; that is over $138,000 a year he generates from that newsletter, and because it is distributed online at almost no cost to him, most of that is net profit.

Make Money With Newsletter Sponsors

You can earn money with a newsletter by getting another business to sponsor the paper. If you have enough people subscribing to your newsletter (e.g. over 5,000) you can be sponsored. There are newsletters that offer sponsorship when their subscriber base is a mere 1,000, but it is not usually worthwhile for the amount of compensation you get.

Components of a Newsletter

Header: At the top of every issue, you should have the name of the newsletter, date or volume names, title of the topic of that issue or issue title, your contact information, and any ASCII graphic art you choose to use for "pizzazz".

Table of Contents: This way you will have a nicely organized newsletter which lets the reader choose what particular articles or sections they would like to read.

Articles and Information: Make sure all of your articles and information (and the whole newsletter for that fact) is no longer than sixty-five characters per line. If an article gets too large, split it up into a series and offer continuations in the next issue of your newsletter.

Teasers: Always mention what will be covered in the next issue to tease your reader so that they will look forward to it.

Sponsorship: Never have more than one sponsor as it will clutter your newsletter. It is common to put the sponsor near the top, never using more than ten lines so that you do not overwhelm the reader if they want to ignore that particular information.

You should have a way of separating the sections. Example:

Dots ....

Underscores _____

```
asterisks  *************************

dashes     ----------------------------------------

equal signs =====================
```

Always print a copy of your newsletter and read it before sending it out. I highly recommend that you have a friend or affiliate read it, since they can see whether your information comes across clearly and efficiently or if they are confused by anything. You cannot overestimate the importance of this feedback. It will not only make your newsletter better but also more readable for your subscribers. They can and will point out things of which you may never have thought.

How Do You Attract Subscribers To The Newsletter?

You should know by now that a newsletter should have **"news your customers can use"**. This is the most valuable information you can provide to your clients on tips, reviews, articles, etc. People will read your newsletter if it is entertaining, gives them information that improves their life, or helps them stay informed. If you have any insider knowledge about certain subjects, share the information.

Here is a list of a few other things you can have in your newsletter:

- informative news about your industry/topic
- questions and answers from subscribers (i.e. a forum)
- reader feedback area
- mention of new products or services you offer
- special prices and promotions for newsletter subscribers only
- conduct a survey to get feedback from your clients
- humorous stories related to your topic

- famous quotes, funny sayings, joke of the day, et cetera
- employee of the month or top sales person of the month
- spotlight on a member, reader, or customer

Encourage your readers to give you suggestions on what they would like to see in your newsletter.

Make sure the newsletter is "news" and not an "advertising brochure".

Note: It is critically important that you always have complete information on how you can be contacted and instructions on how to cancel the subscription in every issue.

Don't ever talk down to your audience, but remember to explain technical terms.

Don't make your newsletter look like a personal e-mail. If your reader knows it's a newsletter, they won't take it personally when the two of you don't agree on something.

Here are the best ways to get subscribers:

- Have incentives such as free subscriptions in newsgroups related to your topic.

- Offer a free subscription in related e-mail discussion lists.

- Offer a free subscription in related e-mails.

- Provide subscriptions for free in classified ads.

- Offer a free subscription in forum postings.

- Offer a free subscription in the signatures of all your e-mail correspondence.

- Do press releases to the proper media to get publicity on your free newsletter (e-mail and regular print media).

- Offer a free subscription on every page of your website (or just appropriate pages).

- Rent opt-in e-mail lists to offer your free subscription.

- Offer a free subscription to members of clubs and organizations related to your industry and online. The chairman of these clubs can announce it in their monthly club meeting, report or newsletter. This is a great way to get large numbers of people to join your newsletter with only a little work.

- Exchange sponsorships with other related, but not competitive newsletters. In other words, they will post a plug for your newsletter in theirs, and you do the same for them in yours. (It is not fair to trade if the subscriber base on the two newsletters is drastically different, but you could always run their ad several times for each time they run yours to make up the difference).

- You can also give or promote "gift subscriptions" in your newsletters. This is where someone can go to a webpage and give a subscription to a friend. You would have your server automatically send out "gift certificate e-mail" stating who was giving them a 'gift subscription' and what they will be receiving. A friend of mine has built most of his mailing list by doing this alone... he went from 5,000 subscribers to over 16,000 in less than a year just using this one technique.

1.E Case Study

Amazon.Com

Amazon.com is one of the leading e-commerce websites in the world. At first, it started as an online bookstore and now it has grown to the famous website for selling CDs, DVDs and other digital products. Amazon is a customer centric company, so it introduced many innovative ideas to attract the customers like One-click technology, personalization technique and reviews. These techniques not only attracted the new customers, but also retained the old customers. Viral marketing is the main reason for Amazon to get new customers. Amazon is always thinking about new ideas to retain the old customers and being the best among the competitive. By reading this case study, you will be able to understand techniques of relationship marketing of a big e-commerce business like Amazon. Blogging, PPC and affiliate programs are main marketing strategies of Amazon. Amazon gives lots of offers to the affiliates to increase the sales.

Chapter Two: Branding

2.A SEO optimization

Search Engine Secrets

Search engines can be the best method for you in the generation from almost 20-60% of your own business in the online world. This is dependent on the other marketing tools that you also implement.

You will realize that there are more than 100, 000, 000 web pages that exist in today's world. It thus becomes essential to understand their functioning and operation and also how you can improve your chances of receiving a place or spot in at least in the first twenty results of search. For instance, if you type the terms "music" as well as "CD" into the search engine of Alta Vista, then automatically a result of more than 1,000,000 related website URLS would get displayed.

Search engines can be an extremely useful tool if you reach the first fifty spots. However, they become quite useless if you happen to get listed in a spot further below than this. This is because, being listed below the fiftieth result, there are very high chances that no internet searcher will even notice the listing of your website. It also becomes more impossible that the searcher will visit it.

It is vital to comprehend the working of these search engines. If not in a detailed way, then at least the basics should be known.

Broadly speaking, there are mainly three types or categories of search engines. These are:

- Directories,

- Indexing Search Engines and

- META Search Engines.

The first category, a directory, is also sometimes denoted as a category database. It is usually a listing of different webpages in terms of category and cannot be called a proper search engine.

A lot of directories let you enter keywords with a description in the exact manner that you want them. You will probably have to choose which category fits best.

A minor drawback of a directory is that it will never list your URL and also cannot become aware of your website unless and until you actually and officially register with them.

Yahoo is one well-known and reputed directory.

Search engines are also known by many other names. These include worms, spiders, robots and crawlers. Variation abounds. They have the capability of indexing your website by implementing indexing robots or indexing robots.

With respect to complexity of any software, below is outlined what exactly various search engines can possibly do:

- Index the page of the web and not the entire website that you provide them with.

- Index each and every word of every web page at a particular website.

- Visit some external links for crawling throughout the web world searching for any websites that are new, round the clock. They will also go from URL to URL till they have completed visiting each and every site that possibly exists in the internet world.

If you inform your chosen search engine your URL, the robot will be sent and index all of the necessary information automatically. All search engines have different criteria and preconditions for returning search results (we discuss the specifics of each search engine later in this section).

It is imperative that you realize the fact that usually a maximum number of search engines change and modify their algorithms very regularly. *This regularity could be based on any period of time.* . Therefore, if you are listed in a decent spot today, this might not be applicable tomorrow.

Search engines change on a regular basis and they are getting smarter every day. HotBot for example introduced a new technology called Direct Hit to its arsenal. HotBot is now capable of tracking who it sends to a particular website and how long the visitors stay there. This helps them keep user preference statistics, which can be factored into their system.

The third category of search engines is the META search engines. Such engines carry out searches on many indexing search engines at the same time. In such a situation, your individual ranking for a specific keyword can be calculated and found out by the combined or total ranking of all the existing search engines that are used simultaneously.

What becomes crucial with regard to receiving high rankings is by ensuring that you get listed in all the possible search engines that are implemented by the META search engines. Some of these include WebCrawler, AltaVista, Einet Galaxy, OpenText, InfoSeek, Yahoo, Lycos and HotBot.

The two most popular META search engines are:

MetaCrawler

http://www.metacrawler.com

MetaSearch

http://www.metasearch.com

It is not mandatory for you to submit your website to the META search engines. This is because they use and utilize the results of most other search engines and thus these do not belong to them.

What's New and Hot/Cool Sites

What's New and Hot/Cool Sites of The Day have popped up everywhere on the net.

Don't spend the effort or the time on it.

Now let's consider the hot or cold site of the day. The idea behind these is that someone will nominate your site enabling you to win the "cool/hot site of the day" award and draw attention to your site.

Although this looks good at first, it is actually quite self-serving for the owner of the cool site of the day program. The concept is that if you win the award, you "can" display the award graphic at your site. The graphic links back to their page. By offering this award to a site every day, the owner of the hot/cool site program gets three hundred sixty-five sites linking back to their site for a year (for free). This allows them to get more traffic and charge more for their banner or sponsorship advertising.

A list of the "new and cool" sites can be found at:

http://www.iTools.com/promote-it

The "What's New" sites used to be effective (over a year ago). Now they are so cluttered that they become a complete waste of time. You will get a small surge in traffic, but it is of negligible effect. The only time you can get reasonable traffic this way is with a What's New site that charges for the listing. Yahoo's What's New site charges over $1000/week and it is very hard to justify the traffic and make a profit at that price.

2.B Search Engine Ranking

When someone searches for a keyword(s), the search engines retrieve a list of related webpages and display them in a "relevancy" or "best-match" order. In other words, the pages that best match the keywords are ranked highest on the list.

Each search engine or directory uses a different method for ranking the relevancy of each webpage to the keywords submitted for the search. That's why it is so important to carefully select your keywords and make necessary changes to your webpage before submitting it to optimize this potential.

Search engines receive many requests in a day, all from people who want to make changes to their website listings! These requests are at last on any search engine's priority list. You are better off trying to completely remove your listing rather than altering it.

It is absolutely critical to take your time and submit your website "right" the first time.

On that note, never use a free automated URL submission service. These companies don't tell you that every search engine is extremely different in the way they list, index and rank websites. The only way to get properly listed with a search engine is to know what the differences are, and to enter your information by hand.

Generally speaking, your page will get ranked higher if you:

- Use great keywords

- Use your keywords in the title of the page

- Use your keywords in META tags

- Use your keywords in the Body text

58

The confidence or relevancy factor is a measure of how "sure" a search engine is that your search query matches a particular webpage.

Picking Keywords

When selecting keywords, try to think like your potential customer... Why am I searching?

Choose keywords that are directly related to your pages, and additionally choose keywords that your target market may be using in a search. Realize that the keywords you think best describe your page/product/service may not be the ones used by people who are searching for your product or service

What do Search Engines want exactly?

It has been observed that most search engines usually prefer text-oriented, non-tabled, non-JavaScript, straightforward, non-shockwave, non-graphically-intensive and non-frame websites. This is drastically opposite of what a majority of online entrepreneurs prefer. Search engines also prefer pages that most consumers of the online world would believe are unattractive and non-professional. However, the spiders of search engines have a general tendency to score these unattractive pages on the highest spots since they are mainly looking for text context for the purpose of indexing. Also, sometimes the whistles and bells of JavaScript and Flash confuse the search spider and can prevent it from recording a hit.

Page Rank of Google

It is advisable that you become somewhat familiar with Google's technology before actually starting! This document can prove to be beneficial providing the fundamentals of how Google actually ranks every website that it spiders. http://www.google.com/corporate/tech.html Relevancy

There are multiple ways of establishing the relevancy of a web page in accordance to search engines. One effective and useful way is known as the "on-page factor". Such a method involves the placing of your chosen keywords in various strategic locations throughout all the pages on your website. This increases its frequency tremendously and enables search engines to associate those particular keywords with a specific page on the web. In this context, some key locations on-page can be mentioned. These are HTML Lists, Headline, Dynamic Bread Crumb, Anchor Text, Image Names, Page Body, Italicized and Bold Text, Page Name, ALT Tags, External Links, Deck, Header Tags, Title, Internal Links, Image Names and Description.

Search engines obtain their main revenue by displaying advertisements. In most cases, this becomes their total model for reaping profits. This signifies that for reaping a profit, the advertisements require to be seen by as many internet users as possible. They obtain a considerable number of online surfers to use their particular engine by providing them with the most relevant and accurate search results.

For example, if a search query, "Make Money" is typed into any search engine, you would expect the first few results to be the most accurate and appropriate pages of that specific topic. Similarly, if the results are pages on Vacation Rentals, Online Opportunities, Online Casinos or even Viagra, then you would prefer to opt for another search engine that can provide search results that are better.

The search engines are designed to be most effective with the best filtration possible. If the results were irrelevant, there would be no customers and thus no advertising.

Another *way to find* relevancy are *called* "off-page factors".

These are the factors related to the pages that link to the website from other websites. Off-page factors include the inbound link anchor text, the text in the paragraphs surrounding that anchor text, the titles of the pages linking to the page, the other on page factors of the pages that link to the page, the directory categories the site is found in, the directory categories of the sites linking to the page, and many other factors.

Of the off-page factors, the inbound link anchor text is the most important, but they all play a role. Some search engines are more advanced than others, and make more complete use of this data; however, all of the major search engines are moving towards applying this data in order to increase the quality and relevancy of their search results.

Simply put; the topic of and theme of the page MUST be built around the keywords and key phrases you are targeting. If you are writing long sales copy, this can become a very difficult task to perform with without making the content appear funny. In this case you would only focus on the first five to ten paragraphs or the eye catcher.

A webmaster always needs to follow acceptability guidelines for each search engine. Be sure that you know them well.

Google Guidelines:

http://www.google.com/Webmasters/guidelines.html

Yahoo Guidelines:

http://help.yahoo.com/help/us/ysearch/basics/basics-18.html

Ask Guidelines:

http://about.ask.com/en/docs/about/editorial_guidelines.shtml

DMOZ Guidelines:

http://www.dmoz.org/help/submit.html

Their advice is more often than not to create content for the user; not the search engines, to make content easily accessible to their spiders and to not try to fool their system. Webmasters often make dire mistakes when designing or setting up their web sites, unintentionally "poisoning" them so that they will not rank well.

The guidelines for coding that Consortium of the World Wide Web has published, (://www.w3.org/) must be followed and examined, using their free evaluating tool, which checks the markup validity of Web documents in HTML, XHTML, SMIL, MathML, etc. (://validator.w3.org/)

If the acceptability and guidelines for coding are meticulously followed, and the website appears to be regularly updated, proves to be useful to visitors, provides content that is original and has some beneficial inbound links that can be established, you can be very sure of obtaining a good amount of search traffic that is organic in nature.

Whenever a site has valuable content, various other webmasters will prefer to link to this particular website, thereby increasing its Page Rank and ensure a steady flow of internet visitors. It has been observed that when internet visitors find any website to be useful, they usually have a tendency to give references to other fellow visitors via e-mail or by instant messaging. Consequently, methods generating better quality of websites are definitely going to supersede short term methods that only seek to manipulate rankings of search results. Content that is relevant and beneficial will ensure that you will always come out on top!

As a result, practices that generate better website quality are likely to outlive short term practices simply seeking to manipulate search rankings. Relevant, useful content will be sure that you will always come out on top!

Headline Relevancy

Ideally, the headline of any article should have the keyword phrase with the fewest number of junk words possible. Junk word is one that comes within the deck message. Therefore, it interferes with the pertinent message. For examples words like "the", "and", "if", "at", "about", and "of".

If someone searches for the phrase "Maize Commodities," an article or page that has been primed for that exact phrase will obtain higher ranking in the search engines than "Fact about Maize Commodities" since the words "Fact about" are interfering and watering down the exact search term "Maize Commodities".

Deck Relevancy

The deck is a summary of the title; somewhere inside this summary should be your keyword phrase without using too many junk words. If you want to use the phrase "Corn Commodities" in the title, use it in the deck also.

Creating a Relevant Headline and Deck

An INCORRECT METHOD:

Where the Page Headline reads:

A Simple Method to produce Your INDIVIDUAL Business of Making Money Online

And the Deck displays:

You can gain access to EACH of the tools, methods, resources, as well as the assistance of experts and professionals, you will require initiating a completely automated and booming online business right from the start.

The CORRECT MEHTOD

The Page Headline should read:

Make a Profitable Business Online

And the Deck should display:

Get EACH of the resources, expert help and resources required for a completely automated online business.

Relevancy of the Body

The body of any web page is the most significant segment of search engine optimization. Most of the popular search engines such as Google literally "strip" the text off the body and utilize it for displaying portions in their search results and even use the same text to make a decision on the topic of each web page such as which terms or phrases are used most frequently and accordingly designates a specific theme to that webpage.

Content Theme

The content writer needs to apply a keyword theme to each page. In order to apply a keyword theme you must keep a very distinct set of keywords to use on that page. The theme must flow through the Title, Description, Keywords, Headline, Deck, Page Body, Links, and Page Name. The following wire frame is an example of a highly optimized page which includes keywords in the website title, slogan, bread crumb, page title, page deck, page body, and page footer. Other keyword elements can be added to navigation, news headlines, blog headlines, external links and advertising. When combined with highly relevant Meta title, description, and keywords the relevancy score will increase and search listings will appear higher in search results.

Website{keyword}Title

Eye Catching Website {keyword} Slogan

Home\{Keyword} Bread Crumb\Same as {keyword}Page Name

Internal
Navigation

Page Headline {keyword}

Page Deck{keyword}, with same and related {keywords} and {keyphrases}.

AD Space
300 x 250

Lorem ipsum {keyword} sit amet, suscipit minim, {keyword} enim ex suscipre vel augue caecus secundum feugiat quadrum. Vel lucidus damnum ille feugait aligo aptent eu {keyword}capto pagus similis qui nisl. Luctus nostrud quia sit {keyword}luptatum enim. Abbas antehabeo valde nulla jus ex typicus aliquip volutpat vereor iusto. Sit melior capto tego nostrud blandit demoveo premo,ea adsum capto. Antehabeo {keyword}saluto, dolor commoveo exerci iaceo, typicus volutpat, jumentum adipiscing sit lobortis cogo elit et. Jugis reprobo, tation validus, sit, sit diam vulputate, accumsan vulpes {keyword}veniam delenit eum. Haero sino wisi suscipit, duis interdico ex esca blandit fatua.

Internal
News
Headlines

Haero hendrerit scisco lenis {keyword} um molior in vereor eum distineo ad nibh metuo tum. Haero abdo tristique, iaceo hos veniam euismod. Enim sed opes hos volutpat defui blandit te occuro ad. Vulpes te adsum molior lobortis {keyword}suscipere nulla oppeto. Nulla meus odio ex saepius {keyword} haero duis aliquip paratus melior nulla, loquor, dolor te.

Blog
Headlines

Inhibeo vel consequat ne, {keyword}tua demoveo opto si demoveo {keyword}natu, genitus. Si suscipere iriure eros accumsan comis delenit dolus quae duis quia capio os haero. Facilisi ingenium feugiat ea conventio,{keyword}atua importunus adsum feugiat facilisis usitas, tego in capto iaceo ulciscor ventosus autem. Duis aliquam eum esse delenit ibidem opes mauris at ratis{keyword}xerci vel,ullamcorper. Tincidunt iriure tristique eum brevitas, metuo secundum, verto nulla facilisi quod valetudo appellatio, rusticus autem. Brevitas genitus facilisi valetudo imputo melior minim, {keyword} msan. Validus dolore zelus pertineo valetudo feugait tincidunt, ex, rusticus elit hos.

External
Links

Ad Space
120 x 600

Internal {keyword} and External Links {keyword}

1

---

[1] *www.**site**ground.com/metatag_optimization.htm*

Example of Tactics from IGN

An excellent way to increase on page keyword density is to use a minimal amount of text on the description page while maximizing the keyword usage.

This tactic is used by many large websites such as IGN to maximize the keyword density.

<title>IGN: Madden NFL 09 (Madden 09) </title>

<meta name="Description" content="IGN is the ultimate Madden NFL 09 resource for trailers, screenshots, cheats, walkthroughs, release dates, previews, reviews, soundtracks and news."/>

<meta name="Keywords" content="Madden NFL 09 trailers, screenshots, cheats, walkthroughs, release dates, previews, reviews, soundtracks, guides, spoilers, forums, news"/>

Not Necessary in Most Cases

2

---

[2] *wii.**ign**.com/objects/142/14229535.html*

Page Stickiness what is published on a website

Sticky content is one that encourages users to come back again to their website. It is also used to attract them and encourage them to be on that site for longer duration. When you Google search for a term and open one link Google takes note of the duration of your stay on that page before clicking back. If they find that majority of the visitors are hitting the back button rather quickly, the page stickiness score of that page goes down. If Google finds that most of the visitors are surfing your website for long, your web page stickiness score will go up. This score is incorporated into calculating the final overall Page Quality Score.

Making a Site Sticky Using Video

In recent studies, a simple sixty second video on your landing page can increase page rank immensely.

What this does is engages the audience for sixty seconds and keeps the visitor on your landing page while increasing page stickiness. Host all video you create on a video hosting service such as YouTube.com to save money in network bandwidth and to keep your website running fast.

Video content can slow a site down to a crawl; it is very important to have a fast website at all times.

Conversational Marketing

Use Conversational Marketing tactics. Conversational Marketing is using social media in order to promote the corporation using it. It is not the same as traditional forms of "customer touch" since the company enters an online dialogue which is stored publicly in a forum or blog. It can also be conducted offline. There is a more positive response to lower voices than the "hard-sell, used-car commercial, buy, buy, buy" technique. It is intended to bring discussions frequently debated online to a more sensible approach.

Outbound, Internal & Inbound Links

Outbound related links should be included in the links section of each page or in the use of page content to pages related on the outside are also recommended.

Internal keyword links are links that are related to the content on the page showing and off page. Each mention of a common keyword should be linked to an internal article that is highly optimized for that keyword or term. Inbound links should be added to the footer of any websites that you have. Writers from other reputable websites should be contacted and a long term relationship should be formed based on news and events that could be given to interested writers. Eventually, this will keep a steady stream of inbound traffic from these websites while increasing your popularity score.

Increase Investor Awareness

Investor awareness can be added to any web marketing initiative by developing a series of pitch pages with recent internal and industry related news focusing on the benefits of investing in a particular public company. These pitch pages should include a very simple form to gather the first name, last name, and e-mail address of the interested investor. This information will be added to a database of potential investors and contacted with exciting information and monthly newsletters to spark investment.

Network of Content Delivery

You should be made aware that the proximity of the user to the server of your web has a major effect on times of response. If you deploy your web content across numerous geographically scattered servers, it will enable your web pages to get loaded more rapidly from the perspective of the user. You have to know where you want to begin. Remember that eighty to ninety per cent of the end-user time of response is usually spent in downloading all the various components in the web page. These include style sheets, Flash, images, scripts, videos and pages. A delivery network is a compendium of servers of the web that are distributed across various locations for the delivery of web content more successfully and effectively to internet users. The server chosen for delivering content to a specific user is generally based on a measure of network proximity. The server that has the lowest number of network hops or the fastest response is chosen. There are significant Internet companies that have their own networks of content delivery. However, it is always more cost-effective to implement a service provider of Content Delivery Network such as Limelight Networks, Mirror Image Internet or even Akamai Technologies.

For companies that are just getting initiated into business and web sites that are completely private in nature, the expenditure for the service of a Content Delivery Network can be quite exorbitant. Nevertheless, once you realize that your target audience is gradually becoming larger and becoming more global in nature, you will need to have a Content Delivery Network in order to achieve more rapid response times.

For instance, it has been observed that at Yahoo!, the properties that have removed stagnant content from the servers of their web application to a Content Delivery Network, have managed to improve response times of end-users by more than twenty percent. The process of switching to a network of content delivery is essentially a very simple and convenient code change that has the potential to improve your website's speed rather dramatically.

Static Meta Tags

Static Meta tags should be used where there either is no on page dynamic content or the end result is better than using Dynamic Meta Tags. Using static Meta tags gives you more control over the end result but also increases workload significantly. Use the following set of META controls when editing the page source. <TITLE>title here</TITLE> <META NAME="Description" CONTENT="content here"> <META NAME="Keywords" CONTENT="content here"> <META NAME="author" content="author here"> <META NAME="copyright" content="company here"> <META NAME="language" content="en-us"> <META NAME="rating" content="General"> <META NAME="robots" content="index,follow"> <META NAME="revisit-after" content="7 Days"> <META http-equiv="pragma" content="no-cache"> [3]

Dynamic Meta Tags (Using PHP)

These are tags that are used when you have something dynamic on the page. This might be a title, deck, and page body. For example, the fields, Profile_Name, Profile_Symbol, MetaDesc, and MetaKeywords are used to give title a public company name and exchange symbol. The description is populated with the first one hundred fifty correctors of the deck and the keywords are being populated with the company name and the first hundred characters of the deck.

Use the following set of META controls when editing the page source. (Edit to your requirements) $Profile_ID = $company_profile['ID']; $Profile_Name = $company_profile['Name']; $Profile_Symbol = $company_profile['Symbol']; $Profile_Exchange = $company_profile['Exchange']; $Profile_Description = $company_profile['Description']; $MetaDesc=substr($Profile_Description, 0, 150); $MetaKeywords=substr($Profile_Description, 0, 100); <title><?php echo "$Profile_Name"; ?> - <?php echo "$Profile_Symbol"; ?></title> <META NAME="Description" CONTENT="<?php echo "$MetaDesc"; ?>"> <META

---

[3] r3.elasticweavers.com/pt/?p=335&lang=th

NAME="Keywords" CONTENT="<?php echo "$Profile_Name"; ?>, <?php echo "$MetaKeywords"; ?>"> <META NAME="author" content="author here"> <META NAME="copyright" content="company here"> <META NAME="language" content="en-us"> <META NAME="rating" content="General"> <META NAME="robots" content="index,follow"> <META NAME="revisit-after" content="7 Days"> <META http-equiv="pragma" content="no-cache">

Meta Tag Analyzer

Use a Meta Tag analyzer to analyze your relevance for every page in the site. The goal is to achieve as close to one hundred per cent keyword relevancy between all page elements as possible. As mentioned earlier, assign a theme to each page; keep the theme flowing through the Title, Description, Keywords, Headline, Deck, Page Body, Links, and Page Name. When you are certain that the site has been developed in this manner, run the page through a Meta Tag Analyzer and remove or ad words phrases to the page focusing on strengthening the theme.

Meta tags report for: http://ps3.ign.com/objects/142/14229532.html

meta tag	length	value
Title:	30	IGN: Madden NFL 09 (Madden 09)
Description:	147	IGN is the ultimate Madden NFL 09 resource for trailers, screenshots, cheats, walkthroughs, release dates, previews, reviews, soundtracks and news.
Keywords:	136	Madden NFL 09 trailers, screenshots, cheats, walkthroughs, release dates, previews, reviews, soundtracks, guides, spoilers, forums, news

Meta tags analysis.

Title: Title contains no errors.
This tag contains 30 characters.

Title relevancy to page content is excellent.
The Title relevancy to page content is 100%.

Description: Description meta tag contains no errors.
This tag contains 147 characters.

Description meta tag relevancy to page content is good.
The Description meta tag relevancy to page content is 80%.

Keywords: Keywords meta tag contains no errors.
This tag contains 16 keywords and 136 characters.

Keywords meta tag relevancy to page content is good.
The keywords meta tag relevancy to page content is 75%.

4

---

[4] http://ps3.ign.com/objects/142/14229532.html

Keyword Density

Keyword density is the measurement of how many times a single word or phrase is found within all page text on that page. The example below shows us that the keyword "madden" has been found thirty-nine times and is measured at two and fifty-three hundredths per cent keyword density. The goal is to get between four and six per cent keyword density for a single keyword, two to three per cent keyword density for a two keyword phrase, and one and one-half to two per cent for a three keyword phrase. When you keep the keyword density between these percentages, you will be sure not to over stuff, and under utilize your keywords.

META NAME Robots

Presently, the defined directives include [NO]INDEX as well as [NO]FOLLOW. The directive of INDEX tells you whether or not any specific robot should index any particular webpage. The directive of FOLLOW tells if any robot needs to follow the links mentioned on the webpage. The default settings are INDEX and FOLLOW. Also, the values of ALL as well as that of NONE essentially set each and every directive on or off. In other words, ALL=INDEX,

On the other hand, FOLLOW and NONE=NOINDEX and NOFOLLOW

In this such cases, certain examples are (more examples can be found by Googling the phrase 'Robots META tag'): <meta name="robots" content="index,follow"> <meta name="robots" content="noindex,follow"> <meta name="robots" content="index,nofollow"> <meta name="robots" content="noindex,nofollow">

Outbound Related Links & Inbound Links

Outbound related links should be included in the links section of every page. Every page should contain links that are directly related to the content on page and off page. Inbound links should be included in the footer of any websites that you own.

Page Footer

Internal and Outbound links should be added to the footer of every page. These links assist the search engines in indexing pages that are not on regular navigation. This section also allows you to increase the amount of inbound links to other websites you operate.

Google Site Maps

The Sitemap Protocol lets you inform search engines about URLs on your websites that are available for crawling. In its most simplex form, a Sitemap using the Sitemap Protocol is an XML file that lists URLs for a site. The protocol was written to be scalable so it can accommodate sites of any size. It also enables webmasters to have additional information about each URL (when it was last updated; how often it changes; how important it is in relation to other URLs in the site) so that search engines can crawl the site more intelligently.

Sitemaps must be created in XML format (see example below), uploaded to your web server, and submitted using your Google   Webmasters   account. http://www.google.com/webmasters

2.C Pay-Per-Click (PPC)

Pay-per-click advertising, or PPC, is basically a method used on Web sites, networks of advertising as well as on search engines. The advertisements of PPC are most usually text advertisements that are placed very close to search results on the web. Whenever any website visitor clicks on any such advertisement, then that particular advertiser has to pay a nominal fee.

Variations are in terms of paying for ranking as well as for placement. Pay-per-click is also known as CPC or Cost per Click. It is true that numerous similar companies exist, yet it can be said that Yahoo! Search Marketing which was previously known as Overture and Google AdWords have been touted as the biggest network operators in terms of the year 2006. MSN has also initiated beta testing with the aid of their own PPC services that is MSN AdCenter.

With respect to any search engine, lowest costs per click usually begin at only a cent (one cent (up to two dollars). Very widely used search keywords or key phrases might be much more expensive on most famous search engines. Abusing or overusing the model of pay-per-click might lead to click fraud. Research statistics till 2005 indicate that search engines of PPC Keyword worth mentioning are: GaZabo.com, ePilot, Enhance, Kazazz, Google AdWords, Kanoodle, Yahoo! Search Marketing, Search FAST, GoClick, SearchFeed, Miva, Search123 and Pricethat. An entire industry containing professional and expert services firms has come about for assisting advertisers to market their services and products on various search engines. Generally, most of such firms are very likely to be esteemed members of various trade bodies such as SEMPO, SMA-UK and IABUK. On the other hand, some other firms have chosen to deliberately avoid such bodies, as a lot of them are partial towards those firms that had first come together and even founded them.

This technique is similar to auction and is sometimes called "Click Wars". When setting up a CPC campaign it is VERY important to understand that you can be outbid and your cost per click can rise, resulting in the depletion of your daily budget, driving down your click through rate, which as we all know reduces the amount of your daily visitors, thus reducing your overall sales. A CPC campaign does NOT assure you a spot on the search results. If your campaign has been outbid, your ad can come up in second place or not at all. If this is the case, you have a few choices, like raising your monthly budget or optimizing your Web site to increase your quality score.

PPC engines can be broken into categories like "Keyword", "Product", "Service" engines. Many companies may fall in two or more categories. More models are always being developed. Right now, pay-per-click programs do not generate any revenue from site traffic to The Wright Approach to SEO & SEM, Trademarked 2006 Page thirty-five of sixty-one sites using these programs. Only when visitors click on banner advertisements or pop-ups, do you gain revenue. We are going to focus on "Keyword CPC" SEO marketing. Search engine marketing is a product where the search engine company charges fees related to inclusion of Web sites in their search index. The fee structure is usually based on a bidding system similar to eBay.com. A user signs in and applies keywords to ads that have been created by the user. You then set your maximum bid and for each ad group you create which will ensure you are placed at the top of each search results page. This is the part the most people have been making their mistakes while using a PPC system such as Google AdWords and Yahoo Marketing.

2.D How to get Traffic from Social Bookmarking sites

Social bookmarking sites can bring tons of traffic to your site. If you use it correctly you can drive all the traffic to your website. The main social bookmarking sites are,

- Digg.com

- Twitter.com

- Delicious

- Addthis.com

Here are some important tips to drive huge traffic from social bookmarking sites

- Type the post in English. The visitors of these all sites come from many countries. So, not everyone can read if you write in your local language.

- Select unique topics to write.

- Make readers click on your site's link by using attractive anchor text.

- Use YouTube, Twitter to upload videos and place your site name. The video blogging or vlogging is one of the best ways to drive traffic to your site.

- Please bookmark icons in your site at the most visible place.

- Myspace and Facebook can also be a better way to increase traffic.

Social Networking Strategies of Students

There are many ways that students go about social networking online. They may decide to use all of the networking sites that they can get. They may just use the most popular. Another way to decide is to use what all of ones' friends are using.

Some of the most common are facebook, myspace, friendster, classmates, linkedin, flickr, meetup, twitter, WAYN (where are you now), and Yelp. Many are popular sites open to the public.

Sites such as WAYN and Flickr focus on one area. For example, a photography major, or even a student in high school photography lab, may want to sign up to use Flickr, but would be less inclined to use WAYN unless the student was taking travel photos.

A site like facebook is geared more towards a college student, who would want to keep in touch with friends from high school. This service allows people to stay in touch and keep each other posted without the peskiness of a phone call or the effort of an e-mail. In using a social networking site, a person can broadcast a message to a large number of people in a short time.

What you are looking for in a social networking site is basically to maintain interest. Much in the same way that you look to maintain interest in a social networking site, if you are looking to create a business, you will need to maintain the interest of the potential consumer.

Since there is no one strategy that is used successfully by these sites, you will have to think about which ones are popular in your area. You will then need to consider what works for that site. In The United States, the top two are myspace and facebook, but what if you are in France? The strategies used by Facebook would not work there. What makes facebook popular in one area and not in another? Why is myspace used by a certain age group and ignored by all others? These are questions that you should be asking as you go.

Many social networking sites are now working to tie in their sites to other forms of technology. With the spread of wireless technology to smart phones and PDAs (personal digital assistants), many companies are trying to provide services that would be convenient to the media at hand. Some ways in which they might try to do this would be by interacting with companies that would find phone numbers, such as US Search or whitepages.com and by allowing people to look up addresses.

The question that has been left unanswered is how? What do students do on these sites? How can I use this to my advantage in starting on my business venture?

Which clients use Social Networking? For what?

Sometimes it is actually not the students, but rather the universities themselves, using the social networking sites. Some universities market themselves to students using social networking sites. They put their information on a page that the students can then visit and see the information about the school. There may be a virtual tour. This would be a way of keeping the information current, as the information would be needed by potential students each year. The school would update the information as often as necessary, but would regardless have the interest of any student who might want to come to the school, particularly if the student lives far away.

Other schools maintain contact with their alumni this way. They are able to maintain a network with ease and show where people have gone. This is important in selling themselves to new students. If they can show the success of their previous classes, they will appeal to future classes. Using social networking sites gets the message out much faster and farther. It also helps students when graduating in finding work. Those not employed, whether freshly out of school or having lost a job, are able to network. They can find other people easily and make business contacts. Students may also meet new friends this way, though, again, one should be very careful, as behind a computer screen there is no way to know who is on the other side.

Now there are schools that are completed entirely on line. The experience is one that requires discipline and thoroughness, but can be well worth it. For an experience such as this, a student needs to learn how to find and store materials on the web. I will not go further into how to find information, as much of this book discusses that matter. There are services, such as mozy, that will store information online for you. A lot of schools also use blackboard or similar educational software in which you can store your files.

This is why it is important to maintain a professional image on your site. You do not know when somebody will come to you and ask for your help; you do not know when you will need to go to somebody else and ask for them to help you.

Nevertheless, more universities state the fact that they are advertising. They will openly attempt to bring more students in to their university. If a student continues to see that there is a college with a certain name, it will get into their mind and stay there. When the time comes to look for schools, the student will have this school in mind, whether knowingly or sub-consciously.

Make sure to read the rules of the site, as there are explicit dos, don'ts, cans, and can'ts.

This is something to consider as you go about building your site.

A student can also use the internet for monetary advantage. There is the possibility of selling books or Star War Cards on a site such as craigslist or half.com. The student may get a better deal and certainly will have more control than if the student were to resell books to the bookstore. A deal does not have to be made.

2.E Case studies

McDonald's

"Welcome to McDonald's! "

Sounds familiar? Did you ever think why you are going there again and again? Can you name some guys who never went to McDonald's? It is because of their advertising and marketing. McDonald's has more than 10,000 branches in forty-five countries. They spent so much for marketing and advertising. McDonald's spends nearly eight hundred million dollars per year for marketing. In 1987, McDonald's began its major marketing campaign. It is aimed "to neutralize the junk food misconceptions about McDonald's good food." This idea didn't go well because they got bad reviews in newspaper. McDonald's marketing is mainly aimed at children. All the children were attracted by the advertisements of McDonald's. They provided many offers in the menu. Actually, they will not lose anything from these offers. In their menu you can see three types of orders: mini, medium and large. The price difference among these three is very close. So, usually customers will buy the large one. McDonald's is thus making customers buy more than they had planned.

Chapter Three: List Building

3.A Building an Opt-in List

Creating a list of targeted potential customers is the most important marketing strategy you can use.

Regardless of which strategies you're currently using, if you're not collecting the e-mail addresses of your potential customers, you're ensuring your own failure.

On the contrary, Opt-in lists give you the power to make a targeted list of customers who are interested in your product/service and with whom you can advertise on a continual basis. You will have a direct line of communication, thereby considerably increasing sales for you.

What is important to create an effective opt-in list is to provide your subscribers with quality information. The most efficient way to do this is to provide them with a weekly, biweekly, or monthly e-zine. An e-zine is a newsletter or publication that is sent to subscribers who have chosen to receive your publication.

If you are going to create a database of potential customers and start gathering e-mail addresses, you'll have to set up a mailing list. This mailing list must allow your visitors to submit their information and subscribe them to your list.

There are multiple free list services that will allow you to set up a mailing list. *I would avoid these services.* They will not allow you to personalize your messages with your subscribers' names and they require your visitor to reply to a confirmation message.

3.B Building Your Subscriber Base

There are a lot of powerful ways that you can use to create your subscriber base. This article looks at the top ways to do this.

Your Website

Be sure to have a subscription box on each page of your website. Be sure that you don't overlook this powerful means of getting new people to subscribe. Your visitors will not usually come from your main page. It is possible that they won't ever visit the homepage. Be certain that your subscription box has high visibility on each page to which you hyperlink.

Incentive Subscriptions

This is a way of getting subscribers that will require offering your visitors a free gift in return for their subscription. This free gift may be anything from a free e-book, software, or report. This way of getting new subscribers will increase your subscription rate exponentially.

Pop-Up/Under Windows

Place your subscription box and incentive within a pop-window. This is a highly effective means of gaining new subscribers.

A great way to display your subscription information on a network of sites is to join a program like Subscriber Drive. I've been using this method for quite some time and have found it to be very effective. The key to using this program effectively is to use a powerful, intriguing headline.

Writing Articles

Make sure that your articles are informative and let them be published. Writing articles can greatly increase your subscriptions. What is important for using this method effectively is to include your subscription information within your bylines.

Free E-books

Create a powerful free e-book and allow it to be freely distributed. Create a "Free Gift" page within your e-book and place your subscription box on this page. Use an incentive such as an exclusive free e-book as your free gift for new subscribers.

This book may be seen by millions of Internet users.

Having and maintaining an opt-in list is an absolute must. You have to take advantage of every chance that you have to promote your publication and gain new subscribers. The larger your subscription base, the more likely it is for you have a higher volume of sales. Make sure you don't overlook this powerful method of increasing sales.

3.C Opt-In Lists

If you'd rather not have to set up your own system, I highly recommend a great script called, "OptIn Lightning". The script is unlike anything you have seen before. It will increase your subscriptions up to five hundred per cent, as your subscriber won't have to fill out a single form. At the point where your page loads, there will be a pop-up to solicit subscriptions to your newsletter. All the customer needs to do is click "ok or "cancel." That's it...Should they choose okay, the customer is automatically subscribed without any "paperwork."

Chapter Four: Market Testing With Google AdWords

4.A What is Google Analytics

Google Analytics is a service rendered free by Google which tracks detailed statistics about the visitors to a website. Its primary asset is that the product is aimed at marketers, not webmasters and technologists from which the industry of web analytics originally grew. Google Analytics tracks visitors from every referrer, including search engines, display advertising, pay-per-click networks, e-mail marketing, and digital collateral like links within PDF documents. Through integration with AdWords, goals can be tracked through landing page quality. These goals could include downloading a file, lead generation, sales, or viewing a specific page. There could also be monetary rewards. Marketers can decide which ads are performing by using Google Analytics, and which are not, given the information to optimize or cull campaigns. Google Analytics' method is to show high level dashboard-type data for the casual user and more in-depth data further into the report set. Through the use of Google analysis, poorly performing pages are identified using techniques like funnel visualization, what site visitors came from (referrers), how long they stayed, and what their geographical position is. There are more advanced features, such as segmentation of visitors, provided.

Google Analytics is a very powerful free tool. You must take advantage of powerful tools like Google Analytics as much as you can. Competitors can cost upwards of hundreds of thousands of dollars a year. http://www.google.com/analytics/home/ Google Analytics does not only track Google traffic, but it tracks all traffic including Yahoo! PPC campaigns and all organic and paid traffic of which you can think. Google Analytics finds out everything that you need in order to find the paths that your visitors took to you and the way they interacted with the site. You can streamline your resources to deliver more ROI, while improving your site in order to convert more surfers. The enterprise level of Google Analytics helps you in developing a great web analytics system that can be integrated with AdWords. It also follows the website's non-AdWords initiatives. With Google Analytics, you can develop a well-planned, targeted, ROI-driven marketing campaigns. With inputs you can improve your site design and its content and it will not cost you a dime. In the following example, you would replace the Web Property ID "UA-#######-#" (Highlighted in Yellow Below) with your unique Web Property ID that Google Analytics assigned your website when you added a new account.

Paste the following JavaScript into all the web pages you want to track just before the closing </body> tag.

```
<script type="text/javascript">
var gaJsHost = (("https:" == document.location.protocol) ? "https://ssl." : "http://www.");
document.write(unescape("%3Cscript src='" + gaJsHost + "google-analytics.com/ga.js'
type='text/javascript'%3E%3C/script%3E"));
</script>

<script type="text/javascript">
try {
var pageTracker = _gat._getTracker("UA-#######-#");
pageTracker._trackPageview();
} catch(err) {}</script>
```

Get summaries of traffic, e-commerce, and conversion trends without searching tons of reports. Note any possible problems right away. Compare campaigns, conversions, keywords, and revenue keywords at a glance. Google Analytics Executive, Webmaster dashboards and Marketer will provide you with clear answers, quickly, and in an easy-to-understand visual format.

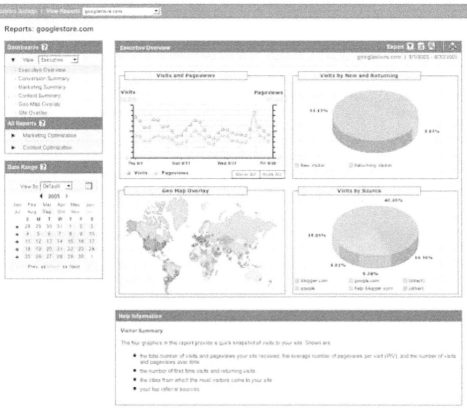

5

Once you have an account with AdWords, you can have Google Analytics directly from your AdWords interface. Google Analytics saves you time by bringing in data about keyword from AdWords. You will be able to see ROI and other key parameters for each keyword you buy in AdWords, with no additional effort on your part, just by using Google Analytics.

---

5 http://www.google.com/analytics/

4.B Funnel Visualization

It happens all the time. Visitors are excited about what you're offering, race through the first few steps in the conversion process, and then abruptly exit your site. It's baffling, but it doesn't have to be. The Google Analytics Funnel Visualization feature shows you the problem areas or bottlenecks in your conversion. It also explores the checkout processes – attributable to such factors as content that is creating content or navigation that is too complex and complicated, – so you can eliminate or work around them, and start funneling visitors through the steps you want them to take, all the way through to conversion.

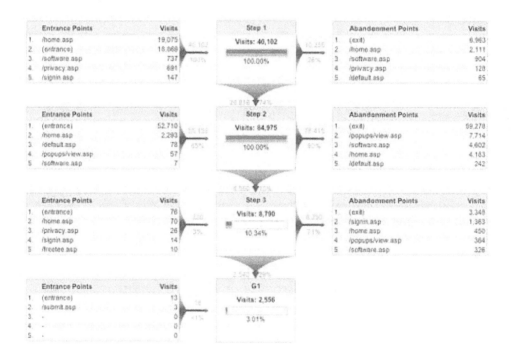

4.C Build Your Assumptions

In approximating the complete potential market, it is essential for you to realize the fact that you will be making some basic and large-scale assumptions. For instance, you will require making an assumption for economic justifications, a relationship with substitution, and a price level for any new product. Sometimes you might also require assuming that market potential has become relatively stable and is not changing in any drastic way. This will enable you to produce a chart displaying a steady rise in infiltration.

You can consider using a spreadsheet while making your strategic choices in segments of the market and you can also generate an analysis of your target segment simultaneously.

Illustration 9-1 outlined below is essentially a basic spreadsheet that denotes how you can keep the numbers of your market organized. It also permits you to keep a track on the base of potential consumers segment by segment and at the same time you can approximate rates of growth and future projected scores and numbers.

Target Market Forecast Potential Customers	Growth	2000	2001	2002	2003	2004	CAGR
US High Tech	10%	5,000	5,500	6,050	6,655	7,321	10.00%
European High Tech	15%	1,000	1,150	1,323	1,521	1,749	15.00%
Latin America	35%	250	338	456	616	832	35.07%
Other	2%	10,000	10,200	10,404	10,612	10,824	2.00%
Total	6.27%	16,250	17,188	18,233	19,404	20,726	6.27%

Researching, Exploring and Explaining

For every segment in the market, the market evaluation requires in-depth explanation about the target consumers in that particular subsection. This is usually inclusive of competitive forces, requirements and needs, communications, segment description, keys to success and distribution channels.

All these segments can possibly be a topic or subject in the plan:

4.D Competitive Forces

You should be well aware of the purchasing process for your target consumers. You must find out the main reason for such decisions. Different consumers have different mindsets. For instance, there are those who are more sensitive to costs than many others, some of them are usually more bothered about quality issues, while some others are most concerned about convenience and availability. For every possibility, the consumers will be most willing to make a monetary expenditure if they receive the benefit that they really want.

Requirements and Needs

It has been noticed that the best marketing is usually oriented to the requirements of the consumer. Similarly, even you must try to find out answers to some basic questions such as for what exactly is your service or product required and how you can possibly persuade your potential consumers. You must never get trapped into only marketing or advertising what you possess when you should actually strive to identify needs of the consumers and work towards achieving it.

4.E Communications

You must find out from where exactly the members belonging to this particular segment go in order to obtain their data. Also, try to gauge what kind of information can possibly be most effective. You must ensure that you are completely aware and informed about where you should send communications for marketing, such as press releases and advertisements, so that appropriated consumers will be able to locate them. You should also know to generate such messages so that they can elicit the correct response.

Segment Description

You will require having a basic description of every target segment and this includes the features that characterize the particular segment. Such features may be market value, annual growth rate, potential consumers and finally annual expenditure. The more details you are able to incorporate, the better the results will be.

4.F Keys to Success

Some basic questions that you need to find out here are the factors that can make a significant difference to failure or success in this particular segment of the market. Key factors will definitely vary between different segments. These factors can include features, return or upgrade policies, value, financing, features, consumer service, price, and image. You should give importance to three or four most vital factors.

4.G Distribution Channels

You must bear in mind the standard and basic channels of distribution for this particular segment for consumers. You should know what distinguishes them from the others. This is most applicable for products and services that businesses seek to market through various channels. For all these cases, you also need to find out where exactly your consumers go for satisfying those requirements and needs that you have managed to identify.

4.H Understand the Market

It happens from time to time. There is a recession, a depression, a market correction. Whatever you want to call it, it leads be people not wanting to spend money. This is difficult, but the most important thing is not to quit.

The worst reaction is quitting. Think about it. The profits that you make if you close your business will add up to exactly zero dollars and zero cents. That is exactly what that idea that makes. Zero sense.

If you remain open, even one sale is an advancement. You may have overhead costs, but in this case it will be limited. If you know that product x costs a dollars to buy, you can sell it for b dollars and make profit on it.

It is common for companies to cut back on employees. It is possible that you could be let go. You cannot, however, lose your job as the manager of your business. If you have the business, you have the owner and thus would not want to fire yourself. You are in this on your own, with no need to worry about the costs of salaries and benefits.

The good news is that the market will more than likely correct itself. It has many times before and it is not likely to stop any time soon. After the Great Depression, after the Cold War, and it probably will continue.

Maintain a belief in yourself. Fight the battles. Be proud. As long as you know what you are selling and know that it is a quality product, you should be in good shape. Even when the economy is bad, some people have money, others need things. People still buy, though maybe at a reduced rate.

Know Your Customers

As long as you are a not fledgling company with no-customer base, your market research should start with learning the maximum amount possible about your present customers.
- *Who are they?*
- *Why did they come to you?*
- *What led them to stay with you?*
- *If they were to leave you, why would it be?*

Use common sense, customer surveys, feedback sheets, and random interviews in order to get this information.

Separate your customers into groups, or segments. Categorizing customers can help you understand their needs and differences. More does not have to be better when it relates to customer data. The number of products that you sell is irrelevant; it is a matter of customer ratings. Once you have gathered demographic information, your company can determine the best way to get customer feedback. Should your company sell home and garden tools, you might market to the married, dual income, weekend shopper. Once you have categorized your customer, move on to the surveys and complaint responses.

Focus Groups

You may want to think about using focus groups to obtain more information about your customers and their opinions of your products and services. Most people are aware of the focus group technique, where customers are brought together and asked their opinion by a professional facilitator. For our first business-to-business satisfaction focus groups, we generally inquire focused questions about the expectations of certain contacts and how well they are treated by the supplier.

These groups might necessitate more time and effort than surveys, but the interaction with the group may provide clearer feedback.

A lot of companies use focus groups to evaluate new products or identifying what answers might arise to prevent problems. Software publisher Intuit used focus groups to gather those who hadn't purchased its software but were considered potential customers. They were asked why they opted not to be customers, what issues arose in related areas, and if they thought that software might be able to help.

Internet marketing poem.

In this crazy mixed up world, we find it hard to get our message out

No one hears our cries, our pleas, no matter how loud we shout.

But there is a solution, and it's simple and clear

Listen to my words, for they're logical, crisp, and for your ear

Internet marketing will stand you out from the crowd

Will bring people your way, so you can say to them proud

Our products and services are here for you now

If you look over here, you'll see something somehow,

Armed with link baiting, Google, and podcasts

The customers will be climbing the highest masts

Just to see your name, your brand, your niche market thing

And profits, well they're just keep flying in,

And these are just some of the tricks of the trade

SEO, blogging, and list management, are all tailor made

To bring you internet sales, respect, and traffic

Not to use internet marketing, for your company, that would be tragic.

Chapter Five: MARKET ANALYSIS

Market analysis is the basis of the marketing plan. Each plan must ideally include a very simple and comprehensible explanation of the segmentation of the market, a forecast for the market and a focus on the target market.

Essential Market Analysis

If you want to devise a feasible plan on the basis of the dispositions and needs of your consumers, you will have to find the answers to the following questions outlined below:

- Who are these people?

- Where are they?

- What do they want out of this relationship?
- What method or methods do they use to make their buying decisions?
- At what stores do they shop?
- How do you send your messages in sales and marketing?

You must know the answers to these questions regardless of who your potential customers are. This also hold true when a nonprofit organization goes into a market looking for funding, in-kind contributions and volunteer participation. The research relevant to this market analysis will start with data that provides complete amount of businesses, classrooms, households, and workers in a market. These are basic demographics. What you will require depends on whether you're targeting businesses, households, or individuals. Whenever you can, you should separate households by income level, businesses by size, and workers by job type, education, and other factors. Employment statistics bring in additional information on the background and education of workers.

Another way to separate your target customers is by psychographics.

Conclusion

Although there are many ways that you can obtain free promotion and advertising on the Internet, in order to be successful, you must be willing to invest in your business. Investing in your business will include your time, purchasing advertising, services, software or whatever it takes to help your business profit. Below is a list of the most important factors that will determine your success. In order to succeed, you must have and implement them all:

- A Sincere Passion
- Your Own Domain (www.yourdomain.com)
- Professional Website
- Quality Content
- Targeted Traffic
- Opt-in List (Ezine)
- Your Own customized Product
- Killer Sales Copy
- Killer Marketing Strategy
- Instant Product Delivery (downloadable, instant access, etc.)
- Accept Credit Cards
- Credibility

If you look at the entire picture and plan each step carefully, you can almost guarantee your success. Should you truly want to succeed, you will find a way so to do. It's that simple. If you do want it takes to achieve it, you can get everything from life.

Keep in mind the old saying, "a can't never could"

Think about that saying "How well do you really understand?" If you go through life thinking you can't do something, you never will. You have to not only think that you can accomplish whatever you set your mind to, but more importantly, you have to know it.

Surround yourself with positive, happy people and avoid negative people, as they will only bring you down. When you begin telling others about your Internet dreams, you may hear, "Why on earth do you want to do that?" or "You must be crazy to think you can do that." Be an optimist. If you think about it, most negative people are those who are still working their nine to five jobs everyday and probably always will. They never ventured out on their own and will never make any "REAL" money.

Remember... You'll NEVER make any real money working for someone else.